v120516
pc: 168
ISBN's: 978-1-944607-00-5 (B&W, CB workbook); 978-1-944607-01-2 (Color, PB workbook)
978-1-944607-02-9 (Digital version—ePub, and MOBI)

TechSmith Camtasia 9:
The Essentials

"Skills and Drills" Learning

Kevin Siegel

"Skills and Drills" Learning

Contents

About This Book

The Author vi

Book Conventions.. vi

Confidence Checks vii

System Requirements vii

Project Files (Data Files)..vii

Download the Data Files vii

How Software Updates Affect This Book.. ix

Contacting IconLogic.. ix

Education Through Pictures.. 2

Planning eLearning Lessons 3

eLearning Development Phases 4

Project Size and Display Resolution.. 6

Design Best Practices... 7

Fonts and eLearning 8

Module 1: Exploring Camtasia

The Camtasia Interface 12

Open a Camtasia Project 12

Explore Camtasia Tools 14

The Media Bin and Library 16

Explore the Media Bin and Library 16

The Canvas and Timeline 19

Preview a Project 19

Module 2: The Camtasia Recorder

Rehearsals 22

Rehearse a Script... 23

Set Recording Options 24

Recording Screen Actions 29

Select a Recording Area 29

Record a Software Demonstration 31

Annotations 33

Add a System Stamp and Caption 33

Recording Confidence Check 37

Recording Effects 38

Add Effects While Recording 38

Module 3: Adding Media

Videos 42

Import a Video 42

Add a Video to the Timeline 44

Video Confidence Check 47

Images 48

Import Images 48

Timeline Confidence Check 49

Multi-Track Projects 50

Add a Track.. 50

Create a Watermark 53

Cursor Effects 54

Add Cursor Effects.. 54

Cursor Effects Confidence Check.. 56

Module 4: Groups, Annotations, Behaviors, and Transitions

Groups.. 58

Create a Group 58

Annotations 60
   Add a Callout 60
   Apply Image Color to Callout Text...62
      Callouts Confidence Check 63
Behaviors 65
   Add a Behavior to a Callout 65
      Behaviors Confidence Check 67
Transitions..68
   Add a Transition to a Group 68
   Modify Transition Timing..69
      Transitions Confidence Check 69

Module 5: Audio
Importing Audio Media 72
   Add Background Music to a Video 72
      Audio Confidence Check...73
   Fade Audio In and Out 74
      Fading Confidence Check 75
Voice Narration...76
   Record Voice Narration 77
Splitting Media 80
   Split a Music Clip 80
      Audio Timing Confidence Check 81
Audio Editing..84
   Rename Tracks 84
   Silence and Cut Audio 85
      Audio Editing Confidence Check 88

Module 6: Sharing
Sharing Videos 90
   Share an MP4..90
   Share to YouTube 94
The Smart Player 96
   Share with a Smart Player 97
Watermarks 99
   Add a Watermark to a Shared Lesson 99
      Sharing Confidence Check 102

Module 7: Extending, Zooming, Trimming, and Interactivity
Extending Frames 104
   Extend a Video Frame 104
      Timeline Confidence Check..106
Trimming..107
   Trim a Video Selection..107
Zoom-n-Pan..109
   Add a Zoom-n-Pan...109
Markers..112
   Add a Marker 112
      Marking Confidence Check 113
TOCs..114
   Add a TOC 114
Hotspots...117
   Add a Hotspot to the Timeline 117
      Hotspot Confidence Check...119

Module 8: Quizzes and Screencast.com

Quizzes 122
   Add a Quiz and Multiple Choice Question 122
   Add a Fill In the Blank Question 126
      Quiz Confidence Check... 127
Screencast.com.. 129
   Share to Screencast.com.. 129
      Screencast Confidence Check 131

Module 9: PowerPoint and Captions

PowerPoint to Camtasia.. 134
   Record PowerPoint 134
Captions 137
   Manually Create Closed Captions 137
   Control Caption Timing 141
      Captions Confidence Check... 142
   Use Speech-to-Text to Create Closed Captions 144

iCONLOGiC

"Skills and Drills" Learning

About This Book

This Section Contains Information About:

- The Author, page vi
- Book Conventions, page vi
- Confidence Checks, page vii
- System Requirements, page vii
- Project Files (Data Files), page vii
- How Software Updates Affect This Book, page ix
- Contacting IconLogic, page ix

The Author

Kevin Siegel is the founder and president of IconLogic, Inc. He has written hundreds of step-by-step computer training books on applications such as *Adobe Captivate, Articulate Storyline, Adobe RoboHelp, Adobe Presenter, Adobe Technical Communication Suite, Adobe Dreamweaver, Adobe InDesign, Microsoft Office, Microsoft PowerPoint, QuarkXPress,* and *TechSmith Camtasia.*

Kevin spent five years in the U.S. Coast Guard as an award-winning photojournalist and has three decades experience as a print publisher, technical writer, instructional designer, and eLearning developer. He is a certified technical trainer, a veteran classroom instructor, and a frequent speaker at trade shows and conventions.

Kevin holds multiple certifications from companies such as Adobe, CompTIA, and the International Council for Certified Online Training Professionals (ICCOTP) as a Certified Online Training Professional (COTP). You can reach Kevin at **ksiegel@iconlogic.com**.

Book Conventions

I believe that learners learn by doing. With that simple concept in mind, IconLogic books are created by trainers/authors with years of experience training adult learners. Before IconLogic books, our instructors rarely found a book that was perfect for a classroom setting. If the book was beautiful, odds were that the text was too small to read and hard to follow. If the text in a book was the right size, the quality of exercises left something to be desired.

Finally tiring of using inadequate materials, our instructors started teaching without any books at all. Years ago we had many students ask if the in-class instruction came from a book. If so, they said they'd buy the book. That sparked an idea. We asked students—just like you—what they wanted in a training manual. You responded, and that methodology is used in this book and every IconLogic training manual.

This book has been divided into several modules. Because each module builds on lessons learned in a previous module, I recommend that you complete each module in succession. Each module guides you through lessons step-by-step. Here is the lesson key:

☐ instructions for you to follow look like this

If you are expected to type anything or if something is important, it is set in bold type like this:

☐ type **9** into the text field

When you are asked to press a key on your keyboard, the instruction looks like this:

☐ press [**shift**]

I hope you enjoy the book. If you have any comments or questions, please see page ix for our contact information.

Confidence Checks

As you move through the lessons in this book, you will come across the character at the right which indicates a **Confidence Check**. Throughout each module, you are guided through hands-on, step-by-step exercises. But at some point you'll have to fend for yourself. That is where Confidence Checks (also known as challenges) come in. Please be sure to complete each of the challenges because some exercises build on completed Confidence Checks.

System Requirements

To complete the lessons presented in this book, you will need the following software and hardware: TechSmith Camtasia version 9; Microsoft Windows 7 SP1, Windows 8, or Windows 10 (Required: 64 Bit versions only); 2.0 GHz CPU with dual-core processor minimum (Recommended: Quad-core i5 processor or better); 4 GB RAM minimum (Recommended: 8 GB or more); 2 GB of hard-disk space for program installation; Display dimensions of 1024x768 or greater.

You will need to download the book's data assets that have been created specifically to support this book (see "Project Files (Data Files)"). Finally, you will learn how to record a PowerPoint presentation on page 146. You will need PowerPoint 2007 or newer to complete those activities.

Project Files (Data Files)

During the activities that appear in this book, pretend that you work for a fictional company called **Super Simplistic Solutions**. As the lead eLearning developer, you must create all of the eLearning content for the company's products, services, and internal processes. During the lessons presented in this book, you will be using Camtasia 9 to create eLearning that might be accessed by learners on a Windows-based computer, an Apple computer, a laptop, or a mobile device (such as a phone or tablet).

Your mission as you work through this book is to learn Camtasia... it's not necessary for you at this point to come up with the eLearning assets needed to create eLearning (such as videos, images, and audio files). That's where our data files come in. The data files support the lessons presented in this book and can be downloaded from the IconLogic website for free.

The process for downloading the Windows data files are below.

Student Activity: Download the Data Files

1. Download the student data files necessary to complete the lessons presented in this book.

   ❏ start a web browser
   ❏ go to the following web address: **http://www.iconlogic.com/pc.htm**
   ❏ from **TechSmith Camtasia** area, click **Camtasia 9: The Essentials** link

   A dialog box may open, asking if you want to Save or Open (or Run) the data files.

□ if you receive a Security message, click the **Run** button

□ click the **Save** button and save the EXE file to your computer

2. After the file downloads, close your browser.

3. Extract the data files.

□ find the **Camtasia9Data.exe** file you just downloaded to your computer

□ double-click the **EXE** to open it (if prompted, click **Run**)

The WinZip Self-Extractor opens.

□ confirm **C:** appears in the Unzip to folder area

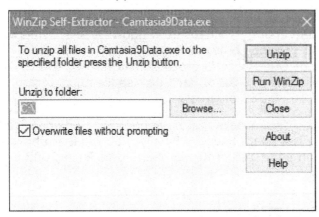

Note: If you are not permitted to extract files to your C drive, click the **Browse** button and Unzip the files to a location that works best for you.

□ click the **Unzip** button

Several files are extracted to your hard drive.

□ click the **OK** button

□ click the **Close** button (to close the WinZip Self-Extractor)

The data files have now been copied to your hard drive (into a folder called **Camtasia9Data**). As you move through the lessons in this book, you will be working with these files. When you have completed the lessons in this book, you can delete both **Camtasia9Data** folder (on the C drive) and **Camtasia9Data.exe** you downloaded to your desktop.

How Software Updates Affect This Book

This book was written specifically to teach you how to use **TechSmith Camtasia version 9.0**. At the time this book was written, Camtasia 9 was the latest and greatest version of Camtasia software available from TechSmith.

With each major release of Camtasia, my intention is to write a new book to support that version and make it available within 30-60 days of the software being released by TechSmith. From time to time, TechSmith makes service releases/patches of Camtasia available for customers that fix bugs or add functionality. For instance, I would expect TechSmith to update Camtasia with a patch or two within a few months of Camtasia 9 being released. That patched version might be called Camtasia **9.01** or **9.1**. Usually these updates are minor (bug fixes) and have little or no impact on the lessons presented in this book. However, TechSmith sometimes makes significant changes to the way Camtasia looks or behaves, even with minor patches. (Such was the case when TechSmith updated Camtasia from version 8.3 to 8.4—several features were changed throwing readers of my books into a tizzy.)

Because it is not possible for me to recall and update printed books, some instructions you are asked to follow in this book may not match the patched/updated version of Camtasia that you might be using. If something on your screen does not match what is showing in the book, please visit the Errata page on the IconLogic website (http://www.iconlogic.com/skills-drills-workbooks/errata-pages-return-policy.html).

Contacting IconLogic

IconLogic, Inc.
1582 Indian Bluffs Dr., Maineville, OH, 45039 | 410.956.4949
Web: **www.iconlogic.com** | Email: **info@iconlogic.com**

Notes

iCONLOGiC

"Skills and Drills" Learning

Rank Your
Skills

Before starting this book, complete the skills assessment on
the next page.

Skills Assessment

How this assessment works

Below you will find 10 course objectives for *TechSmith Camtasia 9: The Essentials*. **Before starting the book:** Review each objective and rank your skills using the scale next to each objective. A rank of ① means **No Confidence** in the skill. A rank of ⑤ means **Total Confidence**. After you've completed this assessment, go through the entire book. **After finishing the book:** Review each objective and rank your skills now that you've completed the book. Most people see dramatic improvements in the second assessment after completing the lessons in this book.

Before-Class Skills Assessment

1.	I can add media to the Media Bin.	①	②	③	④	⑤
2.	I can add a Quiz to a Project.	①	②	③	④	⑤
3.	I can create Captions.	①	②	③	④	⑤
4.	I can share projects on YouTube.	①	②	③	④	⑤
5.	I can create a Watermark.	①	②	③	④	⑤
6.	I can add objects to a project from the Library.	①	②	③	④	⑤
7.	I can create an animation with Behaviors.	①	②	③	④	⑤
8.	I can edit an audio file within Camtasia.	①	②	③	④	⑤
9.	I can add a Zoom-n-Pan to a project.	①	②	③	④	⑤
10.	I can record screen actions using the Recorder.	①	②	③	④	⑤

After-Class Skills Assessment

1.	I can add media to the Media Bin.	①	②	③	④	⑤
2.	I can add a Quiz to a Project.	①	②	③	④	⑤
3.	I can create Captions.	①	②	③	④	⑤
4.	I can share projects on YouTube.	①	②	③	④	⑤
5.	I can create a Watermark.	①	②	③	④	⑤
6.	I can add objects to a project from the Library.	①	②	③	④	⑤
7.	I can create an animation with Behaviors.	①	②	③	④	⑤
8.	I can edit an audio file within Camtasia.	①	②	③	④	⑤
9.	I can add a Zoom-n-Pan to a project.	①	②	③	④	⑤
10.	I can record screen actions using the Recorder.	①	②	③	④	⑤

IconLogic, Inc.
www.iconlogic.com | ksiegel@iconlogic.com

iCONLOGiC
"Skills and Drills" Learning

Preface

In This Module You Will Learn About:

- Education Through Pictures, page 2
- Planning eLearning Lessons, page 3
- eLearning Development Phases, page 4
- Project Size and Display Resolution, page 6
- Design Best Practices, page 7
- Fonts and eLearning, page 8

Education Through Pictures

In a previous life, I was a professional photographer. When I wasn't snapping photos during a five-year tour with the U.S. Coast Guard, I covered media events in New York City as a freelance photographer.

Just about any photographer will tell you that the goal when taking pictures is to capture a story with a few, or maybe just one, photograph. I'm betting that you have heard the saying "a picture is worth a thousand words" more than once. As a professional photographer, I lived those words.

I have spent the bulk of my career attempting to perfect the art of teaching complex concepts to busy, distracted adult learners. I have always attempted to write documentation using as few words as possible and to teach lessons as efficiently as possible.

If you are in the business of educating, you know how difficult the job of writing relevant lesson plans with fewer and fewer words can be. My step-by-step workbooks have long been known for their "skills-and-drills learning" approach. The term "skills-and-drills" learning means different things to different people. For some, it means fast-moving lessons that do not drown a person with unnecessary information. For me, "skills-and-drills learning" means learning something by doing, whatever that something is. It also means learning with a heavy dose of imagery instead of a heavy dose of text.

I learned long ago that people tend to think not with words but with pictures. Here's an example of what I mean.

> *Close your eyes for a second and picture* **three** *in your mind's eye. Open your eyes after a few seconds and read on. (See how precise I am? I know that some of you would have closed your eyes, kept them closed, and then fallen asleep without the last instruction.)*

I wasn't specific when I asked you to picture **three** was I? Because I didn't tell you how to picture *three*, it's a good bet that things such as *three cupcakes*, *three bowls of ice cream,* or *three big boxes of Cap'n Crunch* (everyone knows that the Cap'n is the best breakfast cereal *ever*) flashed into your mind's eye. Maybe a large numeral 3 appeared in your mind's eye—not the word "three." In fact, I doubt that you visualized the word *three*. Why? As I said above, people think in terms of pictures, not words. That's the reason my books usually contain hundreds of screen captures that visually explain a concept that might have taken several paragraphs to explain. And when I do have to explain a concept, I make every effort to minimize the chatter and get right to the point.

Planning eLearning Lessons

By the time you finish this workbook, you will have a better understanding of how to create technically solid eLearning lessons using Camtasia. However, that does not necessarily mean you will create *good* eLearning lessons. If you want to create good, useful lessons, plan ahead by asking yourself the following questions:

☐ **What lessons do I want to make available as eLearning lessons?** (If you are creating an eLearning course that is based on a traditional classroom course, not every lesson will be appropriate for eLearning. In addition, keep in mind that eLearning lessons aren't social events, they are completed by students who are working alone. Any lessons intended for groups may need to be removed from the course or modified to work in an online environment.)

☐ **Have I written a script?** (If you are going to capture a screen process such as the various mouse clicks performed within an application, it is critical that you document the process prior to recording anything using Camtasia Recorder.)

☐ **Do I want my projects to contain images and audio?** (Images and audio enhance the eLearning experience, but where will you find those assets? The Internet is a wonderful resource, but be careful; assets found on the Internet are rarely free and are often protected by copyright laws.)

☐ **Will there be callouts?** (Callouts are written instructions and/or descriptions that describe what is occurring onscreen. Adding callouts in the Editor is easy, but somebody will have to write and proofread them at some point. Keep in mind that while adding content to a callout is easy, Camtasia does not include a spell-check feature.)

☐ **What is the average reading level of my audience?** (Consider your audience and write content that everyone can consume. The lower the reading level of your audience, the longer it will take for learners to read the callouts. In this workbook, you will learn how to set the timing for the callouts. However, you will need to determine the appropriate pace.)

☐ **What font, font size, and colors will I use?** (Because reading text onscreen is not as easy as reading printed content, carefully consider your font choices. Verdana and Calibri are two popular font choices. A dark font color works well when you use a light background.)

When planning projects, keep in mind that the most useful projects contain the following basic elements (you will learn how to add these elements as you move through this workbook):

☐ A Title clip (telling the audience what they are going to learn)

☐ Credits and copyright clip

☐ Narration, music, and other sound effects (as appropriate)

☐ Images and animations (as appropriate)

☐ Some interactivity (such as Hotspots)

☐ An ending clip (reviewing what the audience learned)

eLearning Development Phases

The infographic below offers a visual way to think about the eLearning development process and phases. A larger version of the graphic can be downloaded from www.iconlogic.com/skills-drills-workbooks/elearning-resources.html.

eLearning Development Phases

1 DISCOVERY

Meet with the client. Find out **what they want** in an ideal eLearning course. Who is the **audience**? Define a course **mission statement** for the course in general. You'll also need a mission statement for each lesson in the course. Will the course require **accessibility**? **Audio**? Will it need to be **localized**? What kind of **hardware** will students be using to access the course?

2 DESIGN

Which tool will you be using to develop the content (**Camtasia, Captivate**, **Presenter**, **Storyline**, or perhaps a combination of a couple tools)? **Instructional design**, a **graphical treatment**, and **navigational choices** are now made and implemented.

3 WRITING and/or STORYBOARDING

Now that you have chosen a production tool and decided the overall design of the course, you'll need to **plot out the flow** of the course and **write a script and/or a storyboard**. If the course includes voiceover audio, you'll need a separate (and different) script for that.

4 PRODUCTION

Now it's time to get busy with the **development work** in the selected tool. This includes everything right up to the point of publishing. You'll also **beta test** the lessons in this phase as they are completed.

5 CLIENT APPROVAL

You're almost there! But, before project completion, you'll need to get your **client's approval**. Depending upon how this goes, **you may need to repeat parts of steps two, three, and four**.

6 PUBLISHING and IMPLEMENTATION

This includes not only **publishing locally**, but uploading the content to a **web server** or **LMS (SCORM or AICC)**. Be sure to allow time to work out bugs in this phase.

7 MAINTENANCE

You did a great job! But sometimes changes and updates are necessary. This phase includes **making updates** to the content and **re-posting to the LMS or web server**.

Brought to you by:

iCONLOGiC
www.iconlogic.com

Camtasia Production Time

When I say production time, I'm referring to the actual time you will spend editing a Camtasia project. It may sound like common sense, but the longer each eLearning lesson plays, the longer it will typically take for you to produce it in Camtasia. Many new developers underestimate the number of hours needed to produce eLearning. The following table should help.

Project Size	Number of Production Hours
Small Projects (1-3 minutes of play time)	2-6 hours
Medium Projects (4-6 minutes)	8-12 hours
Long Projects (7-10 minutes)	14-20 hours
Extra-Long Projects (more than 10 minutes)	Consider splitting videos this large into smaller Camtasia projects.

Project Size and Display Resolution

When you create a new Camtasia project or record your computer screen, you'll need to set the project's width and height. For instance, you can create a project and set its size to 800 x 600. That size is perfectly fine for learners who access your content via a desktop computer with a typical monitor (typical meaning a 15-17 inch monitor).

Several years ago, monitors were small and display resolutions were low. In fact, a display resolution of 800 x 600 pixels was common. If you developed eLearning content for a display that small, a project size of 640 x 480 was ideal. A few years later, 1024 x 768 was the standard display resolution, resulting in typical eLearning lessons sized to 800 x 600.

According to **w3schools.com**, the standard desktop screen resolution today is 1366 x 768, and it's trending higher. (You'll find that available resolutions vary from system to system. For instance, I use an HP 22-inch display that doesn't support 1366 x 768. Instead, my closest options are 1360 x 768 and 1376 x 812.)

Because screen resolutions are higher than ever, many eLearning developers are seeking an optimal viewing experience for learners. But what's the ideal size for an eLearning lesson? Unfortunately, there isn't a cookie-cutter answer. The size of the lesson you create depends largely on the size of your display and its resolution. If you are recording a software simulation, the size of your project might be dependent upon the size of the software you're recording (some software cannot be resized and may take up your whole display).

There's more to consider when it comes to project size. What kind of device are your learners using? How big is their display? Is their device typically used vertically (portrait) or horizontally (landscape)? What is the typical size of an iPad? How about a Surface Pro?

If you are creating content for learners using standard desktop computers (Windows or Mac), your 800 x 600 project might look fine. However, if you upload your content to YouTube, 800 x 600 might not look right (you might see black bars on one or both sides of the video, and the video might look distorted during playback).

Selecting an ideal project size is a delicate balancing act between the size of the Camtasia capture area and your computer's screen resolution. When I use Camtasia to create recordings intended for YouTube, I set my computer's screen resolution to the manufacturer's recommendation. Then I set Camtasia's recording area to 1280 x 720. Although I could go higher with my display resolution and capture more of my screen, a higher display resolution tends to lead to smaller text that might be difficult to read.

In addition, I always use the same computer to record all of the videos used in a course. Video cards and display sizes vary from computer to computer and manufacturer to manufacturer. I want my recordings to look consistent so I always use the same computer, same resolution, same Windows theme, and same Camtasia Recorder capture size.

Design Best Practices

Much of what you do in Camtasia will feel similar to what you can do in Microsoft PowerPoint. If you've used PowerPoint you are familiar with adding objects to a slide. In Camtasia, you add objects to the Canvas and use the Timeline to control when those objects are seen by the learner. Unlike PowerPoint, which can contain hundreds of slides, there is only one Canvas in Camtasia, and only one Timeline.

You don't have to be a seasoned designer to produce beautiful and effective Camtasia projects. Here are a few tips to get you started:

- ❏ If you're creating the content in PowerPoint, there are occasions when a bulleted list is the best way to convey an idea. Although PowerPoint uses a bulleted approach to information by default, you do not have to use that format in eLearning.

- ❏ Try splitting the bullets into separate slides with a single image to illustrate each point, or forgo the text and replace it with a chart, diagram, or other informative/interesting image.

- ❏ It is not necessary to have every bit of information you cover on the screen at one time. Encourage your audience to listen and, if necessary, take notes based on what you say, not what is shown on the screen.

- ❏ Few learners are impressed with how many moving, colorful objects each slide contains. When it comes to eLearning, the old saying, "content is King," has never been more appropriate. Ensure each of your screens contain relevant, need-to-know information and that the information is presented as clutter-free as possible.

- ❏ Consider taking more of a photographic approach to the images you use. You can easily find stock photographs on the web using any one of a number of pay-for-use websites. There are many free sites, but keep in mind that to save time and frustration (and improve on the selection and quality), you might want to set aside a budget to pay for images.

Fonts and eLearning

The most important thing about eLearning is solid content. But could you be inadvertently making your content harder to read and understand by using the wrong fonts? Is good font selection really important? Read on to discover the many surprising ways fonts can affect your content.

Some Fonts Read Better On-Screen

eCommerce Consultant Dr. Ralph F. Wilson did a study in 2001 to determine if serif fonts (fonts with little lines on the tops and bottoms of characters, such as Times New Roman) or sans serif fonts (those without lines, such as Arial) were more suited to being read on computer monitors. His study concluded that although Times New Roman is easily read in printed materials, the lower resolution of monitors (72 dots per inch (dpi) versus 180 dpi or higher) makes it much more difficult to read in digital format. Times New Roman 12 pt was pitted against Arial 12 pt with respondents finding the sans serif Arial font more readable at a rate of two to one.

Lorem ipsum frangali puttuto rigali fortuitous confulence magficati alorem. Lorem ipsum frangali puttuto rigali fortuitous confulence magficati alorem.	Lorem ipsum frangali puttuto rigali fortuitous confulence magficati alorem. Lorem ipsum frangali puttuto rigali fortuitous confulence magficati alorem.
Times New Roman 12 pt	Arial 12 pt
520	1123
32%	68%

Source: http://www.practicalecommerce.com/articles/100159-html-email-fonts

Wilson also tested the readability of Arial versus Verdana on computer screens and found that in font sizes greater than 10 pt, Arial was more readable, whereas Verdana was more readable in font sizes 10 pt and smaller.

So should you stop using Times New Roman in your eLearning lessons? Not completely. For instance, you can use Times New Roman for text content that is not expected to be read quickly.

Some Fonts Increase Trust

A 2008 study by Sharath Sasidharan and Ganga Dhanesh for the Association of Information Systems found that typography can affect trust in eCommerce. The study found that to instill trust in online consumers, you should keep it simple: "To the extent possible, particularly for websites that need to engage in financial transactions or collect personal information from their users, the dominant typeface used to present text material should be a serif or sans serif font such as Times New Roman or Arial."

If you feel your eLearning content will be presented to a skeptical audience (or one you've never worked with before), dazzling them with fancy fonts may not be the way to go. You can use fancy fonts from time to time to break up the monotony of a dry lesson, but consider using such nonstandard fonts sparingly. Use the fancy fonts for headings or as accents but not for the bulk of your text.

The Readability of Fonts Affects Participation

A study done at the University of Michigan in 2008 on typecase in instructions found that the ease with which a font in instructional material is read can have an impact on the perceived skill level needed to complete a task.

The study found that if directions are presented in a font that is deemed more difficult to read, "the task will be viewed as being difficult, taking a long time to complete and perhaps, not even worth trying."

The results of the study by Wilson indicate that it is probably not a good idea to present eLearning material, especially to beginners, in a Times New Roman font, as it may make the information seem too difficult to process or overwhelming.

Popular eLearning Fonts

I polled my "Skills & Drills" newsletter readers and asked which fonts they tended to use in eLearning. Here is a list of the most popular fonts:

- ❏ Verdana
- ❏ Helvetica
- ❏ Arial
- ❏ Calibri
- ❏ Times
- ❏ Palatino
- ❏ Times New Roman
- ❏ Century Schoolbook (for print)

Fonts and Personas

If you are creating eLearning for business professionals, you might want to use a different font in your design than you would if you were creating eLearning for high school students. But what font would you use if you want to convey a feeling of happiness? Formality? Cuddliness?

In a study (funded by Microsoft) by A. Dawn Shaikh, Barbara S. Chaparro, and Doug Fox, the perceived personality traits of fonts were categorized. The table below shows the top three fonts for each personality objective.

	Top Three		
Stable	TNR	Arial	Cambria
Flexible	Kristen	Gigi	Rage Italic
Conformist	Courier New	TNR	Arial
Polite	Monotype Corsiva	TNR	Cambria
Mature	TNR	Courier New	Cambria
Formal	TNR	Monotype Corsiva	Georgia
Assertive	Impact	Rockwell Xbold	Georgia
Practical	Georgia	TNR	Cambria
Creative	Gigi	Kristen	Rage Italic
Happy	Kristen	Gigi	Comic Sans
Exciting	Gigi	Kristen	Rage Italic
Attractive	Monotype Corsiva	Rage Italic	Gigi
Elegant	Monotype Corsiva	Rage Italic	Gigi
Cuddly	Kristen	Gigi	Comic Sans
Feminine	Gigi	Monotype Corsiva	Kristen
Unstable	Gigi	Kristen	Rage Italic
Rigid	Impact	Courier New	Agency FB
Rebel	Gigi	Kristen	Rage Italic
Rude	Impact	Rockwell Xbold	Agency FB
Youthful	Kristen	Gigi	Comic Sans
Casual	Kristen	Comic Sans	Gigi
Passive	Kristen	Gigi	Comic Sans
Impractical	Gigi	Rage Italic	Kristen
Unimaginative	Courier New	Arial	Consolas
Sad	Impact	Courier New	Agency FB
Dull	Courier New	Consolas	Verdana
Unattractive	Impact	Courier New	Rockwell Xbold
Plain	Courier New	Impact	Rockwell Xbold
Coarse	Impact	Rockwell Xbold	Courier New
Masculine	Impact	Rockwell Xbold	Courier New

Source: http://usabilitynews.org/perception-of-fonts-perceived-personality-traits-and-uses/

iCONLOGiC

"Skills and Drills" Learning

Module 1: Exploring Camtasia

In This Module You Will Learn About

- The Camtasia Interface, page 12
- The Media Bin and Library, page 16
- The Canvas and Timeline, page 19

And You Will Learn To

- Open a Camtasia Project, page 12
- Explore Camtasia Tools, page 14
- Explore the Media Bin and Library, page 16
- Preview a Project, page 19

The Camtasia Interface

As you work through the lessons in this book, my goal is to get you comfortable with each specific Camtasia area or feature before proceeding. Like any feature-rich program, mastering Camtasia is going to be a marathon, not a sprint. Soon enough you'll be in full stride, creating awesome eLearning content using Camtasia. But before the sprint to the finish line comes the marathon itself. During these first few activities, I'd like to give you a chance to familiarize yourself with Camtasia's workspace. Specifically, you'll start Camtasia, open an existing project, and poke around Camtasia's interface a bit.

Student Activity: Open a Camtasia Project

1. Start Camtasia.

   If this is your first time starting Camtasia, a **Getting Started** project has likely opened by itself, and it's playing. Want to get the preview to stop? Simple enough: on the right side of the screen, there's a playbar centered just beneath the preview. Click the **Pause** button on the playbar (shown in the second image below) to stop the preview (audio and all).

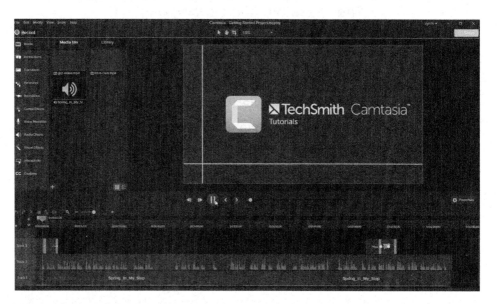

   If this isn't your first time starting Camtasia or you have already created a project or two, I'm betting that the Getting Started project did not open at all. If you're curious to see the Getting Started project, you can open it at any time by choosing **Help > Open Getting Started Project**.

   Note: If the **Help** menu isn't available, you'll first need to create a New Project by clicking **New Project** on the Welcome window.

The picture below is an example of what you will typically see the second time you start Camtasia. By default, there is a **Welcome** window on the screen.

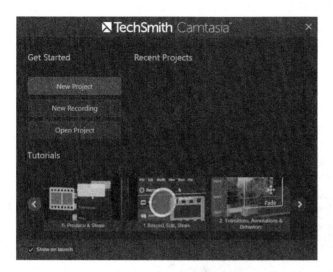

At this point, it does not matter whether or not a project is open. The only important thing is to ensure you have started Camtasia 9.

Note: If you have not yet downloaded your data files, turn to the **About This Book** section at the beginning of this book and work through the **Download the Data Files** activity on page vii.

2. Open a project from the Camtasia9Data, Projects folder.

   ❐ if the **Welcome** window (shown above) is on your screen, click the **Open Project** button; if a Camtasia project is open, choose **File > Open project**

   The **Open** dialog box appears.

   ❐ navigate to **Camtasia9Data** folder on your computer

   ❐ open **Projects > Demo.tscproj**

   The entire screen that you see (from the **File** menu in the upper left to the objects along the bottom of the window) is known as the **Editor**. There are several things to explore within the Editor, which you will do soon enough. First, let's see what happens if you decide to create a new project.

3. Create a new project.

   ❐ choose **File > New Project** (if prompted, don't save the Demo project)

   You are probably used to programs that allow you to open multiple projects concurrently and switch between them. Because you can have only one Camtasia project open at any one time, the Demo project closes when the new project is created.

4. Open a recent project.

   ❐ choose **File > Recent Projects > Demo.tscproj**

   The Demo project should once again be open, ready for you to explore.

Student Activity: Explore Camtasia Tools

1. View the Voice Narration panel.

   ❏ choose **View > Tools > Voice Narration**

   The Voice Narration panel appears in the upper left of the Editor. The panel is used to record your voice (assuming you have a microphone attached to your computer). You will learn to record voiceover audio beginning on page 77.

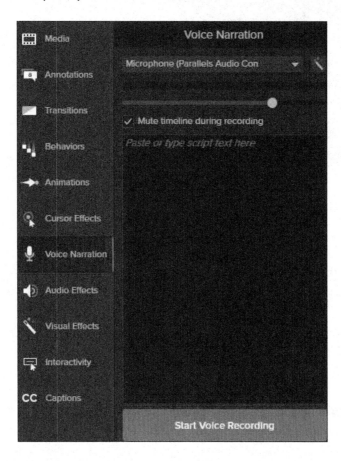

   You can also access Voice Narration via the panel at the far left of the Editor.

2. Show the Annotations panel.

   ❏ from the list of tools at the left, click **Annotations**

   There are six types of Annotations that allow you to help grab the learner's attention (including Callouts, Arrows and Lines, Shapes, Sketch, and Keystroke images). You will learn to add Annotations beginning on page 60.

3. Show the Transitions panel.

   ☐ from the list of tools at the left, click **Transitions**

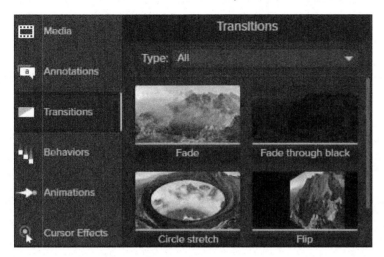

Transitions give you the ability to move from one part of your lesson to another using professional animation effects. You'll learn how to add Transitions to a project beginning on page 68.

Next you will explore the Media Bin and the Library.

The Media Bin and Library

Every new Camtasia project has a Media Bin... but it's empty. You import assets, such as images, into the Media Bin as needed. Once assets are imported into the Media Bin, you can add them to the Camtasia Timeline. Each project contains its own unique Media Bin. Unfortunately, you cannot share Media Bins across projects. By contrast, the Library comes preloaded with assets provided by TechSmith including animations, icons, and music. Library assets are available to use in any project right away. All you need to do is select the asset(s) and add it to the Timeline.

Student Activity: Explore the Media Bin and Library

1. View the Media Bin.

   ❐ from the list of tools at the left, click **Media**

   There are two areas that make up the Media panel: the Media Bin and the Library (you can easily click between them).

   ❐ ensure that the **Media Bin** is selected

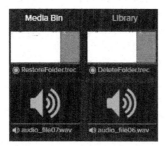

   There are a several assets in this project's Media Bin including videos, images, and audio clips.

   The default view for the Media Bin is Thumbnails, which is nice if you want a decent-sized preview of the Media Bin assets. However, many developers prefer the organized look and feel of the Details view.

2. Change the Media Bin view from Thumbnails to Details.

   ❐ at the bottom right of the **Media Bin,** click the **Details** icon

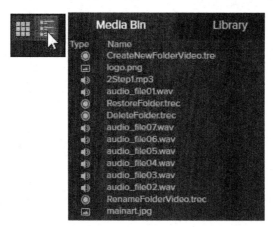

3. Change the Media Bin view from Details back to Thumbnails.

   ❏ at the bottom right of the Media Bin, click the **Thumbnails** icon

   You will learn how to add assets to the Media Bin beginning on page 42.

4. Show the Library panel.

   ❏ on the Media panel, click **Library**

   The Library takes the place of the Media Bin. By default, there are several folders within the Library containing myriad images, animations, and audio files. You can create your own folders and import your own assets into the Library.

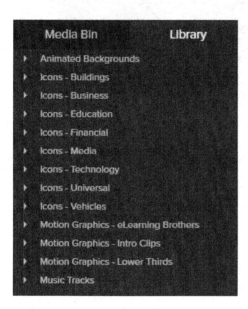

5. Explore a Library folder.

   ❏ from the Library, click the triangle to the left of **Music Tracks**

   The folder opens and displays several assets.

   It is simple to add any of these assets to your project—a drag and drop is all it takes. You will get a chance to do that later (page 75). For now, let's continue the Camtasia tour.

6. Preview a Library asset.

☐ on the **Library**, right-click any music track and choose **Preview**

A preview window opens and, assuming you have speakers or a headset, you will hear the music. (You can preview images and video is the same manner.)

☐ close the Preview window

You will learn how to add music from the Library to a project on page 75.

The Canvas and Timeline

The Canvas, which is at the right of the Editor, offers an excellent way to position screen elements and preview the project as you're working. As you preview a project via the Canvas, you'll be able to use the Timeline to keep track of what's happening in your project and when.

The Timeline is at the bottom of the Editor. As its name implies, the Timeline is used to control the timing of objects added to the Canvas. For instance, using the Timeline, you can force objects such as images or videos to appear at the same time, or you can force one object to appear as another goes away. You'll learn to use both the Canvas and Timeline as you move through lessons in this book. For now, you'll use the Canvas to preview the assets added to the Timeline of the demo project.

Student Activity: Preview a Project

1. Preview the project.

   ☐ on the **Canvas**, click **Play** tool

   As the lesson plays on the Canvas, notice that a thin line and strange-looking object track across the Timeline. The object is known as the Playhead (it has both a green and a red square, which you will learn about later). The Playhead and thin line show you where the preview is in relation to the Timeline. You will learn to work with the Timeline as you progress through the lessons in this book.

   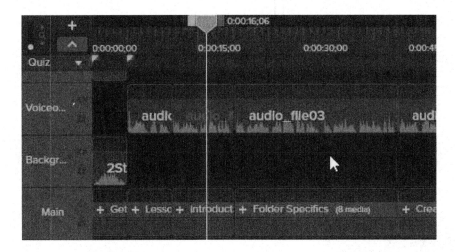

2. Detach the Canvas.

   ☐ choose **View > Canvas > Detach Canvas** (you can also find this option via the **Canvas Options** drop-down menu located just above the Canvas)

The Canvas detaches from Editor. You can now position the panel anywhere on your display that you like.

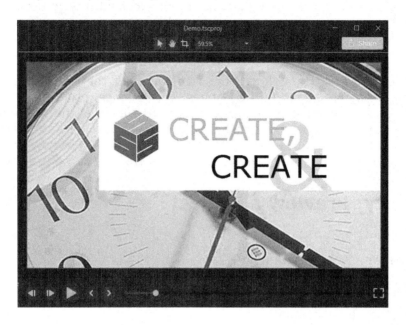

3. Explore Full Screen Mode.

   ❏ with the Canvas detached, click the **Full Screen** button (in the lower right of the Canvas)

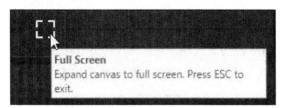

   While in Full Screen mode, you can see the lesson but not the Camtasia interface.

4. Exit Full Screen mode.

   ❏ press [**esc**] on your keyboard

5. Attach the Canvas.

   ❏ from the top of the detached Canvas, click the **Canvas Options** drop-down menu (shown below) and choose **Attach Canvas**

   The Canvas reattaches to the upper right of the Editor.

6. Exit Camtasia (**File > Exit**).

   There is no need to save any changes made to the Demo project (if prompted).

iCONLOGiC

"Skills and Drills" Learning

Module 2: The Camtasia Recorder

In This Module You Will Learn About:

- Rehearsals, page 22
- Recording Screen Actions, page 29
- Annotations, page 33
- Recording Effects, page 38

And You Will Learn To:

- Rehearse a Script, page 23
- Set Recording Options, page 24
- Select a Recording Area, page 29
- Record a Software Demonstration, page 31
- Add a System Stamp and Caption, page 33
- Add Effects While Recording, page 38

Rehearsals

You have been hired to create an eLearning course that teaches new employees at your company how to use **Notepad**. One of the lessons you plan to record using Camtasia includes how to change the page orientation within Notepad.

Here is a sample script showing the kind of detailed, step-by-step instructions you need to create or receive from a Subject Matter Expert (SME). You are expected to perform each step written below in Notepad.

> Dear Camtasia developer, using Notepad, record the process of changing the Page Orientation from Portrait to Landscape and then back again (from Landscape to Portrait). Create the recording using a computer display resolution and screen capture size that you think is best. Thanks. Your pal, the Subject Matter Expert.
>
> 1. From within Notepad, click the **File** menu.
>
> 2. Click the **Page Setup** menu item.
>
> 3. Click the **Landscape** orientation button.
>
> 4. Click the **OK** button.
>
> 5. Click the **File** menu.
>
> 6. Click the **Page Setup** menu item.
>
> 7. Click the **Portrait** orientation button.
>
> 8. Click the **OK** button.
>
> 9. Stop the recording process (you're done).

The script sounds simple. However, you will not know what kind of trouble you are going to get into unless you rehearse the script prior to recording the process with Camtasia. Let's run a rehearsal, just as if you were a big-time movie director and you were in charge of a blockbuster movie.

Places everyone... and quiet on the set...

Student Activity: Rehearse a Script

1. Start Notepad.

    Notepad is a common accessory on PCs running Windows. If you're using Windows 7 or newer, the easiest way to find Notepad is to Search for the program.

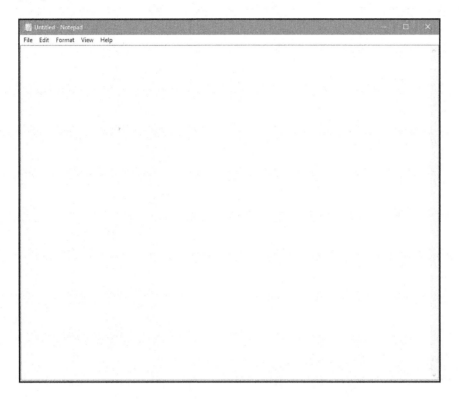

2. Rehearse the script.

    ❏ using Notepad (not Camtasia), click the **File** menu

    ❏ click the **Page Setup** menu item

    ❏ from the **Orientation** area, click **Landscape**

    ❏ click the **OK** button

    ❏ click the **File** menu

    ❏ click the **Page Setup** menu item

    ❏ click the **Portrait** orientation button

    ❏ click the **OK** button

    Hey, look at that! The script worked perfectly... no surprises. You are now ready to work the exact steps again. Only this time, you will record every click that you make. During the recording process, Camtasia creates a video of the entire process.

Student Activity: Set Recording Options

1. Start the Camtasia Recorder 9 tool. (The Recorder tool is installed in the same folder as Camtasia. It can be started like any other application.)

   There are two main things to notice on your display. First, there is a green, dashed box that is likely the size of your display (meaning it's really big). Second, there is a Recorder control panel containing four menus (Capture, Effects, Tools, and Help). There are two main groups on the control panel (**Select area** and **Recorded inputs**). Last, there's a large, red **rec** button.

2. Select the Capture File format and File options.

   ❑ on the Recorder control panel, choose **Tools > Options**

   The Tools Options dialog box opens.

   ❑ ensure that the **General** tab is selected

   ❑ from the **Saving** area, **Record to** drop-down menu, ensure **.trec** is selected (it is selected by default)

   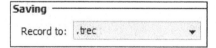

   A trec file is the default Camtasia recording file format. It's a proprietary file format that can be opened only with Camtasia. Generally speaking, this format works very well with Camtasia.

❒ at the right of the dialog box, click the **File options** button

❒ from the **Output file name** area, select **Automatic file name**
(if necessary... this option is the default and is likely already selected)

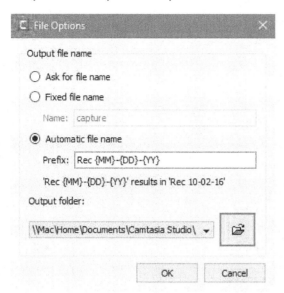

With the **Automatic file name** option selected, you won't be prompted to name the video when you are finished recording. Instead, the recording will automatically be named, saved (by default, recordings are saved to your Documents folder inside a Camtasia Studio folder), and imported into the Camtasia Editor where it can be previewed.

❒ click the **OK** button

3. Select the Capture options.

❒ still working on the **General** tab, ensure your Capture settings match the picture below

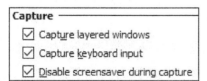

Here is what the **Capture** options do (if you have additional options not shown in the image above, you can leave them as is):

Capture layered windows. On by default. You will be able to capture translucent or irregularly shaped layered windows.

Capture keyboard input. On by default. If you are using the trec file format, Camtasia Recorder captures keys as you press them on your keyboard and automatically creates callouts for you. The callouts can be edited, deleted, moved and resized in Camtasia during production.

Disable screen saver during capture. On by default. You should enable this option when you are creating long, unmonitored recordings.

4. Select the Program options.

☐ with the Tools Options dialog box open, select the **Program** tab

☐ ensure your options match the picture below

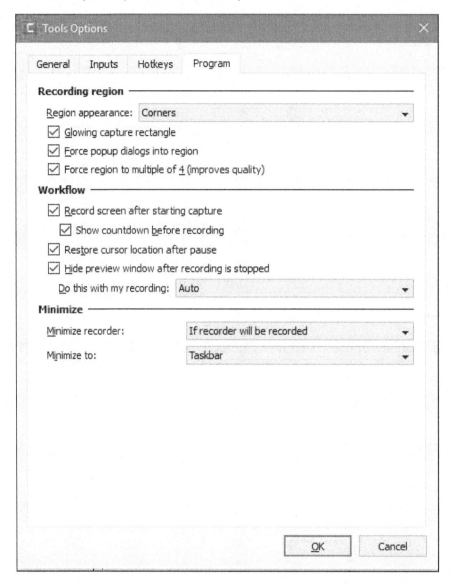

Here is what some of the options do (you can always refer to the Help menu for more information).

Glowing capture rectangle. On by default. Makes the green corners around the recording area flash.

Force popup dialogs into region. On by default. Ensures dialog boxes and other popup windows appear within the recording area.

Force region to multiple of 4. On by default. Prevents errors when viewing videos created with codecs, such as Microsoft Video 1.

Record screen after starting capture and **Show countdown before recording.** Both on by default. Once you click the red **rec** button, the capture process begins. However, you'll have a few seconds to get ready, thanks to a countdown you will see just before the recording begins.

Restore cursor location after pause. On by default. Restores the cursor to the position on the screen prior to the pause. This allows you to seamlessly continue the action in the recording prior to the pause. You must press [**F9**] to pause and resume the recording to use this option.

Hide preview window after recording is stopped. On by default. Select this option if you don't want to preview the captured video after recording.

Minimize recorder. This prevents Camtasia from creating a video of itself.

Minimize to. By default, the recorder will be minimized to your Taskbar if it's going to be in your way during the recording process.

5. Set the Record/Pause Hotkey.

   ❏ with the Tools Options dialog box open, select the **Hotkeys** tab

   ❏ click the **Restore defaults** button

   ❏ from the list at the left, select the **Record/Pause** option

   ❏ from the drop-down menu at the right, notice that **F9** is selected

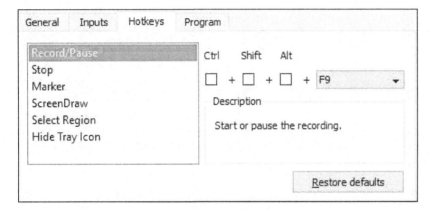

6. Set the Stop Hotkey.

   ❏ select the **Stop** option from the list at the left

   ❏ from the drop-down menu at the right, ensure **F10** is selected

The remaining Hotkeys, although important, won't impact the video you are about to create. Understanding that [**F9**] starts or pauses the recording process and that [**F10**] stops the recording process is important to keep in mind for the activity that follows.

   ❏ click the **OK** button

7. Disable your camera and microphone.

    ☐ on the Recorder control panel, choose **Capture** and ensure that both **Record audio** and **Record webcam** are **deselected**

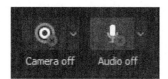

I'm a fan of including audio in eLearning. In my experience, voiceover audio almost always enhances the learner experience. However, I'm not a fan of recording audio *during* the video creation process with the Camtasia Recorder. It's not that you can't record quality audio. The concern is that unless you've done a fair amount of voiceover work, you'll likely end up replacing the audio later in Camtasia. When teamed with the concentration needed to capture screen actions, most people tend to talk too fast, too slow, or flub way too much to record decent audio. You'll learn later that it's easy to import, record, and edit audio from within Camtasia (refer to the lessons beginning on page 71).

What about capturing yourself with your video camera? Nope... I'm not a fan of that either. Ask yourself this question: "Is it really necessary to insert myself into this lesson?" The answer will likely be no. If you do elect to record yourself (recording yourself is often referred to as creating a selfie-video), are you sure you're dressed appropriately? Yes? Okay, but what about what's behind you? Is there a poster in the background that's inappropriate? If you look good and the background is great, what about the lighting around you? What about your camera angle? Because there's much to consider when it comes to selfie-videos, consider not doing them. Besides, if you have awesome existing videos of yourself, you can insert them into Camtasia later (see page 42).

But enough about recording audio and video. Let's go ahead and record your first demonstration.

Recording Screen Actions

When you record screen actions using Camtasia, you should pretend you are using a video recorder and creating a movie (you're both the director and the producer). During the recording process, everything you do is recorded exactly as you do it. Every delay, every good click, bad click, right-click, double-click... everything is recorded. If you move your mouse too fast and race through a series of steps, the resulting video will play back the cursor speed in real time. Move too slowly, and your learners will tear their collective hair out as they watch the cursor slowly move across the screen.

In the steps that follow, you'll select a recording area and then record the process of changing the Page Orientation in Notepad.

Student Activity: Select a Recording Area

1. The Camtasia Recorder should be running. In addition, the Notepad window should be open.

2. Select a recording area.

   ❑ on the Recorder control panel, **Select area** section, ensure **Full screen** is selected

   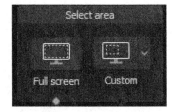

   Full screen means that the recording area is set to record your entire screen. However, unless you are recording a very large application, smaller recording sizes are usually preferred.

   ❑ on the Recorder control panel, select **Custom**

   The Select area expands and displays a Dimensions box.

   ❑ from the middle of the Recording area, drag the four-headed arrow over to the Notepad window (dragging the four-headed arrow allows you to position the Recording area anywhere you want on your display)

   ❑ on the Recorder control panel, **Dimensions** area, click the **Lock** tool to **unlock** Aspect Ratio

With this option disabled, you will be able to easily resize the Recording area as you see fit... but keep in mind it is advisable to select Standard recording sizes such as you'll find in the **Custom** drop-down menu (such as 1024x768 or 800x600).

☐ resize the Notepad window to any size you like

☐ resize the Recording area so that the entire Notepad window is within the Recording area

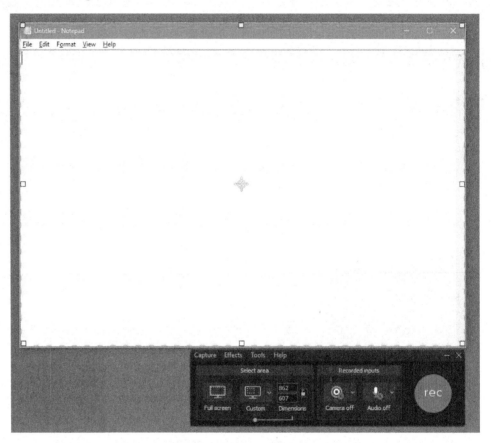

And now, on with the recording!

Student Activity: Record a Software Demonstration

1. Record a software demonstration.

   ❐ on the Recorder control panel, click the red **rec** button

   You'll see a three-second countdown.

   ❐ before the counter gets to zero, position your mouse pointer in the center of the Notepad window

   After the counter disappears, your every move (and the time it takes you to move) is being recorded.

   ❐ moving steadily (not too fast), move your mouse pointer to the **File** menu

   ❐ click the **Page Setup** menu item

   ❐ from the **Orientation** area, click **Landscape**

   ❐ click the **OK** button

   ❐ click the **File** menu

   ❐ click the **Page Setup** menu item

   ❐ click the **Portrait** orientation button

   ❐ click the **OK** button

2. Stop the recording process.

   ❐ press [**F10**] on your keyboard

   Once you press the Stop recording hotkey on your keyboard, the recording process terminates, and several things happen in rapid succession. First, the Camtasia Recorder application automatically closes. Second, Camtasia starts, and a new project is automatically created. Last, the demonstration you just recorded is automatically added to the Camtasia Media Bin and inserted onto the Timeline.

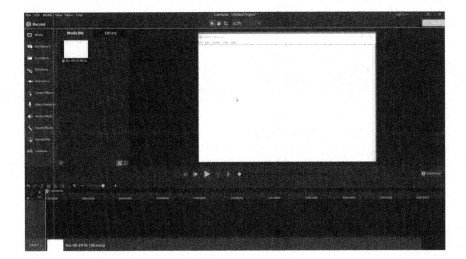

If you'd like to watch the demonstration you recorded, you can use the controls at the bottom of the Canvas window to play and rewind the video.

3. View the location of the recording.

❏ on the **Media Bin**, right-click the recording and choose
   Open File Location

The Camtasia Studio folder opens automatically. By default, all of the
recordings you create are saved to this folder. You can change this location in
the Camtasia Recorder via **Tools > Options > General > File options**.

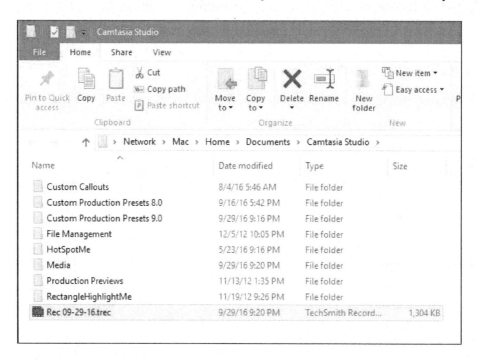

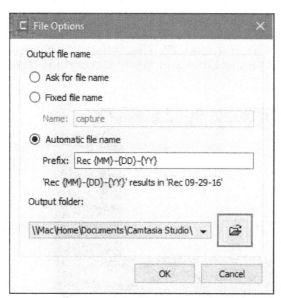

4. Close the window and return to the Camtasia project.

Annotations

Annotations (informational text) can automatically be added to a Camtasia video during the recording process. There are two types of Annotation: System Stamp and Caption. Camtasia can insert one of two system stamps (time/date and elapsed time) into the recording. The stamp is imprinted into the video file and is visible to learners. Captions are frequently used to include a copyright notice or other text message that you want to appear on the video.

Student Activity: Add a System Stamp and Caption

1. Ensure that you are working within the untitled Camtasia project you created during the last activity.

2. Start the Recorder from within Camtasia.

   ❐ from the top left of the **Editor**, click **Record**

   The Camtasia Recorder reopens. The Recorder typically remembers your last settings so unless you closed Notepad, the application should be showing within the Recording Area.

3. Add a System Stamp.

   ❐ on the Recorder control panel, choose **Effects > Options**

   The Effects Options dialog box opens.

   ❐ on the **Annotation** tab, select **Time/date**

   ❐ if necessary, deselect **Elapsed time**

   A preview of the date and time format appears just below the check boxes.

   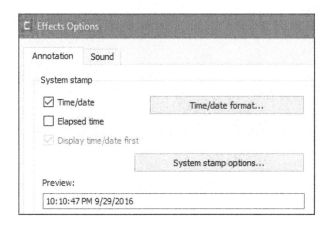

4. Specify a Time/Date Format.

   ❏ click the **Time/date format** button

   ❏ from the Display area, select **Date only**

   ❏ click the **OK** button to return to the Effects Options dialog box

5. Set the System Stamp font.

   ❏ working on the **Annotation** tab, click the **System stamp options** button

   The System Stamp Options dialog box opens.

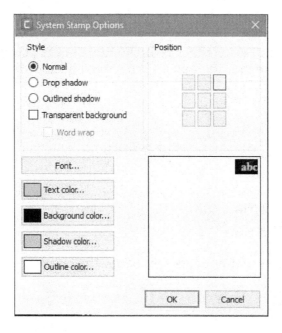

   ❏ click the **Font** button

   ❏ change the Font to **Verdana** and the Size to **10**

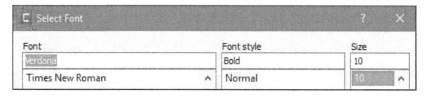

   ❏ click the **OK** button

   You are returned to the System Stamp Options dialog box.

6. Set the System Stamp position.

   ❒ from the **Position** area in the upper right of the dialog box, select the lower left square (this will position the System Stamp in the lower left of the video)

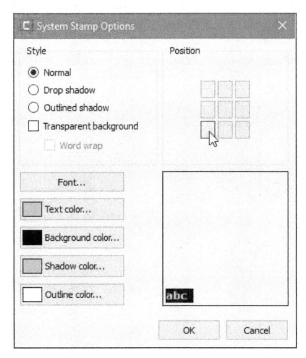

   ❒ click the **OK** button

   You should now be back in the Effects Options dialog box.

7. Add a Caption.

   ❒ click in the Caption text field and type: **This is a sample lesson. Not for resale.**

   ❒ deselect **Prompt before capture**

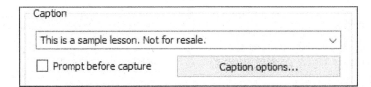

8. Set the Caption font.

   ❒ click the **Caption options** button

   The Caption Options dialog box appears.

   ❒ click the **Font** button

   ❒ change the Font to **Verdana** and the Size to **10**

   ❒ click the **OK** button

9. Set the Caption Text and Background color.

❐ click the **Text color** button

The Select color dialog box opens.

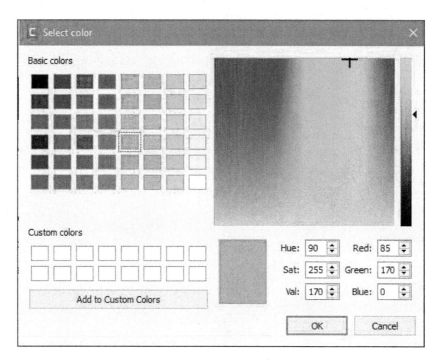

❐ select any color you like

❐ click the **OK** button

❐ click the **Background color** button

The Select color dialog box opens again.

❐ select any color you like

❐ click the **OK** button

10. Set the Caption position.

❐ from the Position area, select the upper right square (this positions the Caption in the upper right of the video)

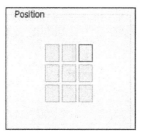

❐ click the **OK** button twice (to close both open dialog boxes)

---

11. Enable the System Stamp and Caption effects.

   ❏ on the Camtasia Recorder, choose **Effects > Annotation > Add system stamp**

   ❏ on the Camtasia Recorder, choose **Effects > Annotation > Add caption**

   Both commands should now be selected (there should be a check mark next to both).

Recording Confidence Check

1. Click the **rec** button on the Recorder control panel.

2. Record the process of changing the page orientation like you did during your first recording session.

3. When finished, stop the recording process.

   Your new recording will be added to the Camtasia Media Bin.

4. Double-click the new recording to open a preview window.

5. Play the preview and notice that you can see both a System Stamp and Caption on the video.

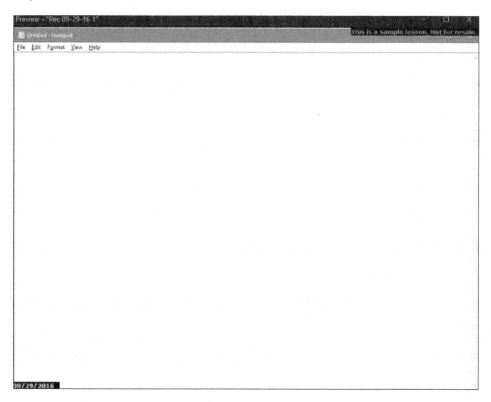

6. Close the preview window.

Recording Effects

Starting in the next module, you will learn how to add all kinds of media to an eLearning lesson that will help grab the learner's attention including images, behaviors, and music. However, using Camtasia's Effects Toolbar, you can add several attention-grabbing visuals while you are recording your video.

Student Activity: Add Effects While Recording

1. Ensure the Effects toolbar is enabled.

   ❏ from the top left of the Editor, click **Record**

   The Camtasia Recorder reopens.

   ❏ on the **Recorder control panel**, choose **Effects > Annotation** and turn off both Add system stamp and Add captions

   ❏ on the **Recorder control panel**, choose **Tools > Recording toolbars**

   ❏ select **Statistics**, **Effects**, and **Duration**

   ❏ click the **OK** button

2. Record a video and add screen drawings.

   ❏ click the **rec** button

   After the 3-2-1 countdown, the Statistics, Effects, and Duration tools should appear on the Recording toolbar (on some of my systems, the tools appear on their own; on others, I had to click in the middle of the Recording toolbar to coax the tools to appear... you may have to play with this a bit to display the tools).

   ❏ select the **ScreenDraw** tool

Drawing tools appear. You can select from among frames, lines, highlights, ellipses, and even a pen.

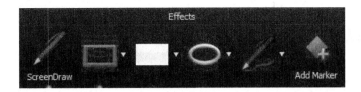

❏ select any of the tools and draw some shapes within the Notepad window

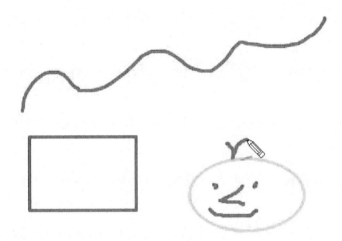

On the Recorder control panel, notice that there are also **Duration** and **Statistic** counters.

❏ when finished drawing, stop the recording

3. Preview the video in Camtasia.

4. When finished, exit Camtasia (there is no need to save the untitled project).

5. Close the Notepad application.

Notes

iCONLOGiC

"Skills and Drills" Learning

Module 3: Adding Media

In This Module You Will Learn About:

- Videos, page 42
- Images, page 48
- Multi-Track Projects, page 50
- Cursor Effects, page 54

And You Will Learn To:

- Import a Video, page 42
- Add a Video to the Timeline, page 44
- Import Images, page 48
- Add a Track, page 50
- Create a Watermark, page 53
- Add Cursor Effects, page 54

Videos

During the first module of this book, you were introduced to the tools that make up Camtasia, opened a Camtasia project, and explored the Editor interface (page 12). Then you used Camtasia Recorder to record screen actions (beginning on page 29). Now you'll create an eLearning lesson from scratch using the Camtasia Editor.

The first thing you will learn to add to the new project is video. When it comes to importing video files, you can import any of the following video formats:

☐ **trec** (a recording created with newer versions of the Camtasia Recorder, which you learned how to use on page 29),

☐ **camrec** (a recording created with older versions of the Camtasia Recorder)

☐ **mp4** or **mpeg** (a file format created by the Moving Picture Experts Group, which was designed to compress video into a digital format)

☐ **avi** (Audio Video Interleave, an early Microsoft video file format), wmv (Windows Media Video developed by Microsoft)

☐ **mov** (Apple's proprietary format that plays using only Apple's "Quick Time" player).

Student Activity: Import a Video

1. Start Camtasia.

2. On the **Welcome window**, click **New Project** or, if a Camtasia project is already open, choose **File > New Project**

3. Import a video.

   ☐ from the top left of the Editor, click **Media** to display the Media Bin

   ☐ on the **Media Bin** panel, ensure you are in **Thumbnail** view

   ☐ click **Import Media**

The Open dialog box appears. Any supported video file you can access from your computer can be imported using this dialog box.

❐ from the Camtasia9Data folder, open the **Video_Files** folder

This folder contains videos created with an older version of the Camtasia Recorder.

❐ open **CreateNewFolderVideo**

The video appears in the Media Bin.

4. Preview the imported video.

❐ on the **Media Bin**, double-click the video you just imported

The imported video opens in a Preview window.

You will learn later in this book (page 90) that a Camtasia project needs to be rendered (otherwise known as publishing or sharing) so that it can be accessed by your learners. If you were to render or share the project now, the video on the Media Bin would *not* be included in the shared video. If you intend for imported media to be included in a shared video, you need to ensure that the media is added to the Timeline. Let's do that next.

5. Close the preview window. (Leave the Camtasia project open.)

Student Activity: Add a Video to the Timeline

1. Add a video to the Timeline.

   ❏ on the **Media Bin**, right-click the video and choose **Add to Timeline at Playhead**

On the Timeline, the video you added is represented by a horizontal bar.

Now that there is an asset on the Timeline, if you share your project so it can be accessed by your learners (page 90), there would actually be something for them to see. And because you have content on the Timeline, you can take advantage of the preview options via the Canvas.

2. Preview a project on the Canvas.

   ❏ on the **Canvas**, click the **Play** button to see the video again

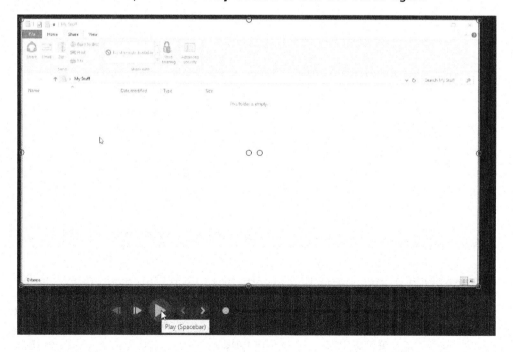

The video plays just like it did via the Preview window. However, there's also an object that moves along the Timeline and it's synchronized with the

preview. This object is known as the **Playhead**. You'll spend plenty of time working with the Playhead later.

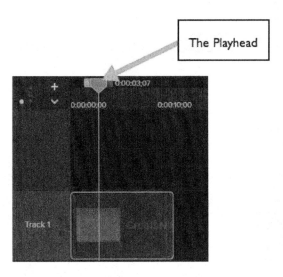

3. Save the project.

   ❏ choose **File > Save**

   ❏ name the project **CreateNewFolder** (ensure you are saving to **Camtasia9Data**, **Projects** folder) and then click the **Save** button

   A dialog box appears with some essential messages that are often overlooked. First of all, a Camtasia project contains a **tscproj** extension. Second, these kinds of projects can be opened only with Camtasia 9 or newer. Third, you are reminded that you must produce your video if you'd like learners to be able to use it (something you will learn to do later). Notice that there is a **Don't show again** check box. This is one of those times where getting rid of a dialog box might be a good idea. If you can remember that you'll need to produce your videos before anyone can use them, there is no need to acknowledge this dialog box in the future.

   ❏ if you'd like, select **Don't show again**

❑ click the **OK** button

Note: You can reset any **Do not show this again** check boxes by choosing **Edit > Preferences** and, on the **Advanced** tab, selecting **Show all tip dialogs** from the **Tips** area.

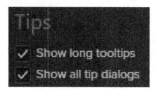

4. On the **title bar** of the Camtasia Editor, notice that the saved project has a **tscproj** extension.

If I were going to give you a pop quiz right about now, a couple of questions you might come across would be about extensions for Camtasia assets. During the past few modules, you have learned that videos created with Camtasia Recorder have a trec extension; and you've learned that Camtasia projects have a tscproj extension. Got it? (There's no quiz coming up by the way... so breathe easy.)

Video Confidence Check

1. Ensure that the **CreateNewFolder** project is open.

2. On the **Timeline**, right-click the video you just added and choose **Delete**.

   The video is removed from the Timeline. Now that it has been removed from the Timeline, it would no longer appear in a produced lesson. However, notice that the video remains in the Media Bin. Items in the Media Bin remain available for you to preview and add to the Timeline, but items in the Media Bin will not appear in a produced video unless they have been added to the Timeline.

3. Ensure the **Playhead** is positioned as far left of the Timeline as it will go.

4. Right-click the video in the Media Bin and choose **Add to Timeline at Playhead** to add the video to the Timeline again.

5. On the Timeline, zoom closer to the video in Track 1 by clicking the **Zoom timeline in** tool.

   The ability to Zoom closer to Timeline objects will prove useful later when you need to split the audio or synchronize the video with other Timeline objects. You can always use the **Zoom timeline out** tool to move farther away from the Timeline or drag the slider (the circle between the plus and minus signs).

6. Save the project (choose **File > Save Project** or press [**ctrl**] [**s**] on your keyboard).

Images

Few things enhance an eLearning lesson better than quality images. Camtasia supports many of the standard graphic formats, including bitmaps, GIFs, and JPEGs. You can learn about the different graphic formats with a quick Internet search (one site that I find helpful is **Dan's Data** (www.dansdata.com/graphics.htm). If you don't have ready access to photographs and other images, I've had great success with BigStockPhoto.com and iStockPhoto.com. Both of these sites offer awesome collections of inexpensive, royalty-free images. You'll also find some wonderful eLearning assets on the eLearning Brothers website (www.elearningbrothers.com).

Student Activity: Import Images

1. Open an existing Camtasia project.

   ❑ choose **File > Open project**

   ❑ open **Camtasia9Data >Projects > ImageMe.tscproj**

   This project is identical to the one you were just working on. It has the CreateNewFolderVideo in the Media Bin and on the Timeline.

2. Import an image to the Media Bin.

   ❑ choose **File > Import > Media**

   ❑ from the Camtasia9Data folder, open the **Image_Files** folder

   ❑ open **logo.png**

   The logo image appears in the Media Bin.

3. Import another image.

   ❑ choose **File > Import > Media**

   ❑ from the **Image_Files** folder, open **mainart.jpg**

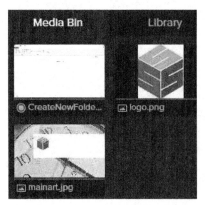

Timeline Confidence Check

1. On the Timeline, drag the **CreateNewFolder** video to the **right** approximately one-half inch (this leaves space to the left of the video for the mainart image).

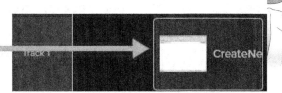

Drag the Timeline object to the right to make room for other track items at the left.

2. Drag the **mainart.jpg** image from the Media Bin to the beginning of Track 1 on the Timeline.

3. On the Timeline, drag the **CreateNewFolder** object **left** until it bumps up against the mainart image).

4. On the **Canvas**, click the **Play** button to preview the project.

   Notice that the mainart image appears on the Canvas and then, after a few seconds, the image disappears and the video showing how to create a new folder plays.

   If you want to have one Timeline object appear, then disappear, and then another Timeline object appear, all you have to do is add objects to the Timeline horizontally and move them (or stretch them) on the Timeline to control when they appear and for how long. However, if you want to have multiple Timeline items appear at one time, you'll need multiple Timeline tracks... something you'll learn about next.

5. Save your work.

Multi-Track Projects

You've added two assets to the Timeline (the video and the mainart image). Both objects appear on a single Track called Track 1. You can easily add additional tracks to the Timeline. Once you have multiple tracks, you can precisely control when multiple Timeline objects appear on the Canvas and how items appear on the Canvas in relationship to other Timeline items. For instance, you can add your corporate logo to a Timeline track above the video track and create a watermark effect... perfect for corporate branding.

Student Activity: Add a Track

1. Ensure that the **ImageMe** project is open.

2. Insert a new track.

   ❏ on the top left of the Timeline, click **Add a track**

   On the Timeline, notice that Track 2 has been added above Track 1. Because Track 2 is above Track 1 on the Timeline, anything you add to Track 2 appears to float (stacked) above anything on Track 1 when viewed on the Canvas.

3. Add an image to the Track 2.

   ❏ if necessary, drag the Playhead left to the beginning of the Timeline

   ❏ on the Media Bin, right-click **logo.png** and choose **Add to Timeline at Playhead**

Only one object can be positioned on a track at a particular time point on the Timeline. Because the Playhead is positioned at 0.00 time and there is an object on Track 1 at that time point, the logo is automatically added to the next available track (in this instance, the beginning of Track 2). If you hadn't manually added the second track prior to adding the image to the Timeline, the track would have been added automatically.

4. Change when the logo appears on the Timeline.

   ❏ on **Track 2**, position your mouse pointer in the **middle** of the **logo**

   ❏ **drag the logo** right until its **left edge** lines up with the left edge of the CreateNewFolder on Track 1

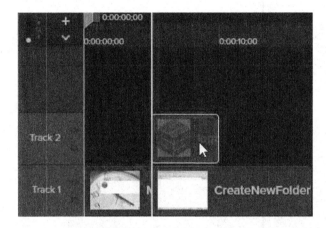

5. Position the Playhead and preview a portion of the video.

   ❏ on the **Timeline**, double-click the CreateNewFolder **video** object

   The Playhead, which indicates the current frame selected (or time point) on the Timeline, should now be positioned just before the CreateNewFolder video.

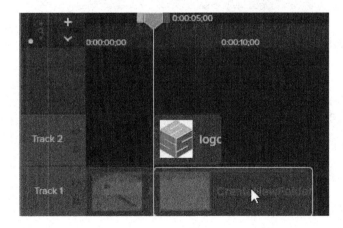

   ❏ on the **Canvas**, click **Play**

   On the Canvas, notice that the logo image appears in the middle of the video by default. In addition, the logo disappears long before the video is finished.

6. Save your work.

7. Extend the play time for the logo.

   ❏ on the Timeline, use your mouse to point to the **right edge** of the logo object

   Note: If you are very close to the Timeline, it might be helpful to zoom out a bit before working with the Timeline objects.

   ❏ when your mouse pointer changes to a **double-headed arrow**, drag the **right** edge of the logo object **right** until the logo's bar ends when the video ends (as shown in the images below)

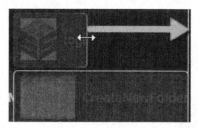

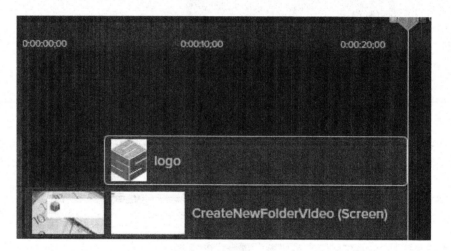

8. Preview the timing changes.

   ❏ on the Timeline, double-click the **CreateNewFolder** video object

   On the Timeline, the Playhead should once again appear just before the **CreateNewFolder** video on the Timeline.

   ❏ on the **Canvas**, click the **Play** button to preview the project

   On the Canvas, notice that the logo image sticks around for the duration of the video. (It's too big, and it doesn't work all that well in the middle of the video... but you'll fix those issues next.)

9. Save your work.

Student Activity: Create a Watermark

1. Ensure that the **ImageMe** project is open.

2. Display the Properties panel.

   ☐ on Track 2, right-click the **logo** and choose **Show Properties** (if you see **Hide Properties** instead, you can move to the next step)

   At the **right side** of the Editor, notice that there's a Properties panel.

3. Make the logo smaller.

   ☐ on the **Properties** panel, drag the **Scale** slider **left** to change the Scale to **50%** (if you find it difficult to get to exactly 50, type **50** into the Scale field at the right)

4. Lower the Opacity of the logo.

   ☐ on the Properties panel, drag the **Opacity** slider **left** to change the Opacity to **40%** (again, if you find it difficult to get to exactly 40, type **40** into the field at the right)

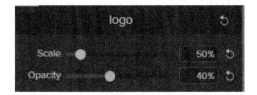

5. Change the object's video position.

   ☐ on the Canvas, drag the logo near the bottom right of the background

6. Save your work.

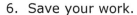

Cursor Effects

Earlier in this module you added a video to the project that demonstrates the process of creating a new folder on a computer (page 42). You've previewed that video several times during this module, so it's likely that you have already noticed that in the video the mouse, through the process of creating a new folder, moves from one part of the window to the next. As the cursor moves, there are no click sounds or visual effects to draw the learner's attention to the clicks. Unfortunately, you're working with an existing video, so there's no way to alter the cursor's behavior... or is there? Because the video was created with the Camtasia Recorder, and it's a .trec file, the cursor can be modified in the Editor (you can easily add such enhancements as click effects and click sounds).

The ability to alter the cursor properties in the Camtasia Editor is an exclusive feature available only in trec and camrec videos created by the Camtasia Recorder. If you import any other type of video into the Editor (such as an mp4 video), you cannot modify the cursor properties.

Student Activity: Add Cursor Effects

1. Open an existing project.

   ❏ choose **File > Open project**

   ❏ open **Camtasia9Data >Projects > MouseMe.tscproj**

2. Preview the lesson.

   ❏ on the **Timeline**, double-click the **CreateNewFolder** video to move the Playhead to the beginning of the video

   ❏ on the **Canvas**, click the **Play** button to preview the project

   As the video plays, pay particular attention to the mouse cursor. It's moving around the screen just fine, but you can't hear any mouse clicks. During the steps that follow, you'll add both a click sound and a visual effect.

3. Add a Left Click effect to the cursor.

   ❏ on the **Timeline**, double-click the **CreateNewFolder** object to move the Playhead to the beginning of the video (and select the video on the Timeline)

   ❏ from the list of tools at the left, click **Cursor Effects**

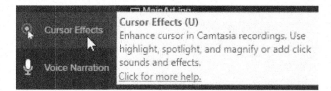

   The Cursor Effects panel opens. Using this panel, you can add visual effects to the mouse throughout the video.

❏ from the top of the Cursor Effects panel, select **Cursor Effects**

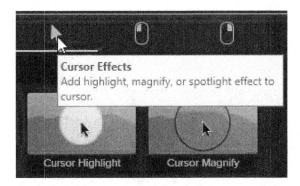

❏ right-click **Cursor Highlight** and choose **Add to Selected Media**

The effect is instantly added to the selected video. You can tell an effect has been added to media via the **Show effects** arrow beneath the video on the Timeline.

4. Preview the video.

❏ on the **Canvas**, click the **Play** button to preview the video

You've just added a nifty highlight effect to the mouse. *How cool is that?*

Note: You can control the appearance of the effect (such as the Opacity) via the **Properties** panel at the right of the Canvas. In the image below, I changed the Opacity of my highlight to 30%, making it easier to see the text behind the highlight.

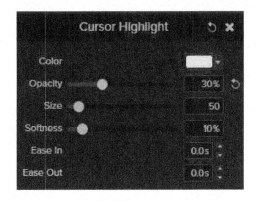

Cursor Effects Confidence Check

1. On the Timeline, click **Show effects** just below the video.

2. Right-click the Cursor Highlight effect and choose **Delete** to remove it.

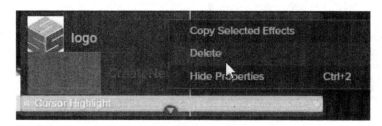

3. Spend a few moments adding different effects to the video's cursor.

   Note: Experiment with the **Left Click** effects on the Cursor Effects panel.

4. Preview the video to see your new cursor effects.

5. When finished, save your work.

Module 4: Groups, Annotations, Behaviors, and Transitions

In This Module You Will Learn About:

- Groups, page 58
- Annotations, page 60
- Behaviors, page 65
- Transitions, page 68

And You Will Learn To:

- Create a Group, page 58
- Add a Callout, page 60
- Apply Image Color to Callout Text, page 62
- Add a Behavior to a Callout, page 65
- Add a Transition to a Group, page 68
- Modify Transition Timing, page 69

Groups

As you add media to the Camtasia Timeline things are likely to get a bit, shall we say, frenzied. You can have several Timeline tracks, and each track can contain multiple items. Because you can use the Timeline to precisely control how long each item appears on screen, changing the timing of one object can easily foul up its relationship to objects on other tracks. Given how complex Timeline relationships can become, you'll appreciate Camtasia's ability to group objects. Rather than moving an individual object on the Timeline (only to realize you left a related object on a different track behind), you can group objects and move everything in the group at one time.

Student Activity: Create a Group

1. Open **AnnotateMe.tscproj** from the **Camtasia9Data** Projects folder.

2. Extend the Duration of an image.

    ❏ on the Timeline, right-click the **mainart** object (the first object in Track 1 and choose **Duration**

    A Duration panel appears.

    ❏ change the **Duration** to **20** seconds and press [**enter**]

The mainart image on the Timeline stretches and pushes the CreateNewFolder video right. Because it is located in a different track, the logo you are using as a watermark on the video does not move.

If things stay as they are, it looks like you will have to potentially move multiple objects every time you change an object's timing. This is a perfect use-case for grouping. In the next step, you'll group the CreateNewFolder video and the logo. Once the objects are grouped, timing changes made to objects left of the group push the group right.

3. Undo the last step.

    ❏ choose **Edit > Undo** (or press [**ctrl**] [**z**])

    The timing for the mainart image should be back to 5 seconds.

4. Create a group.

  ❏ on the Timeline, select the **CreateNewFolder** video in Track 1

  ❏ press [**shift**] and select the **logo** in Track 2 (then release [**shift**])

  Both the video and the logo should now be selected.

  ❏ right-click either of the selected objects and choose **Group**

  The objects have now been grouped. The logo, which was in Track 2, has been moved into the new group on Track 1.

5. Name the group.

  ❏ right-click the new group and choose **Rename Group**

  The group's default name, Group 1, is selected.

  ❏ change the group's name to **Creating Folders** and press [**enter**]

6. Extend the Duration of the mainart image again.

  ❏ on the Timeline, right-click the **mainart** object (the first object in Track 1 on the Timeline) and choose **Duration**

  ❏ change the **Duration** to **30** seconds and press [**enter**]

  This time the entire group moves right on the Track to accommodate the extended playtime of the image.

7. Remove empty tracks.

  ❏ at the left of the Timeline, right-click the words **Track 2** and choose **Remove Track**

8. Save your work.

  Note: To ungroup objects, right-click a group and choose **Ungroup**. If you'd like to see the objects that make up a group, click the **plus sign** in the upper left of a group to expand the group.

Annotations

Annotations are typically used to explain a concept being shown on screen or to highlight something. There are several types of Annotations, including Callouts (shapes that can contain text), Arrows, Lines, Shapes, Motions, and Keystroke Callouts. In the Demo project you opened at the beginning of this book, there are several Callouts synchronized with the voiceover audio. One of the Callouts from that project is shown in the image below (the words CREATE and FOLDERS). During the activities that follow, you will add and then format a few Callouts.

Student Activity: Add a Callout

1. Ensure that the **AnnotateMe.tscproj** project is open.

2. Insert a Callout.

   ☐ on the Timeline, double-click the mainart image to move the Playhead to the far left of the Timeline

   ☐ from the list of tools at the left, click **Annotations**

   The Annotations panel opens.

   ☐ on the **Annotations** panel, click **Callouts** (the first Annotation type)

   ☐ from the **Style** drop-down menu area, choose **Legacy**

   ☐ double-click the **last Callout** in the **last row** to add it to the Timeline and the Canvas

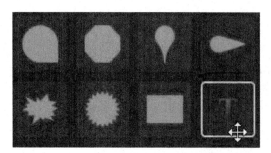

3. Format the Callout's text.

   ☐ with the Callout selected on the Canvas, open the **Properties** panel (if necessary)

   ☐ at the top of the Properties panel, click **Text Properties**

   ☐ change the Font to **Verdana**

   ☐ change the text color to **Black**

   ☐ change the Font size to **80**

   ☐ change the **Alignment** to **Left**

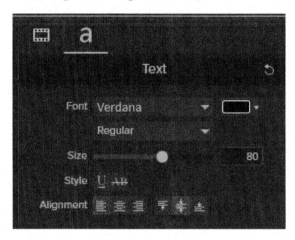

4. Add the Callout text.

   ☐ replace the existing text in the Callout with the words **CREATE FOLDERS**

   ☐ resize and position the Callout on the Canvas similar to the image below

5. Save your work.

Student Activity: Apply Image Color to Callout Text

1. Ensure that the **AnnotateMe.tscproj** project is open.

2. In the Callout, highlight the word **CREATE**.

3. Pick up color from an image and apply it to selected text.

   ❏ at the top of the Properties panel, click **Text Properties**

   ❏ from the color area, select the **Select color from image** tool

   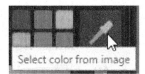

   ❏ using the **Select color from image** tool, click the green "S" on the logo

   The color you clicked with the **Select color from image** tool is applied to the highlighted text in the Callout.

4. Save your work.

Callouts Confidence Check

1. Click in front of the word **FOLDERS** and press [**enter**].

2. Press [spacebar] a few times to indent the word **FOLDERS**.

3. On the Timeline, right-click the Callout and **Copy** it to the clipboard.

4. On the Timeline, position the Playhead just to the right of the Callout.

5. **Right-click** the existing Callout and choose **Paste**.

   Because you positioned the Playhead prior to pasting, the pasted Callout is pasted after the existing Callout on Track 2.

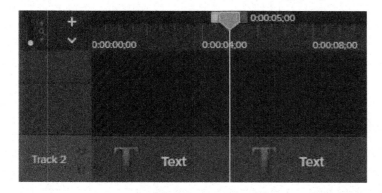

6. Double-click the new Callout and change the word **CREATE** to **RENAME**.

7. On the Timeline, position the Playhead just to the right of the second Callout.

8. **Right-click** the Callout and choose **Paste**.

9. Double-click the new Callout and change the word **CREATE** to **DELETE**.

10. Change the word **FOLDERS** to **RESTORE**.

11. Save your work.

12. Create a **new** Camtasia project.

13. Spend a few moments adding some of the other Annotations to the project. (There is no need to save the project, so play as much as you'd like.)

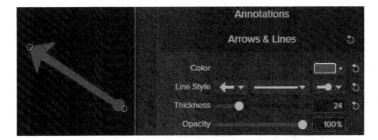

As you add the Annotations, notice the formatting options available to you on the Properties panel. You'll find that the options vary depending upon the type of Annotation you're working with.

Behaviors

Behaviors, also known as Effects, are animations that are typically used to add some visual excitement to your project. Behaviors can be attached to images, video clips, and several types of Annotations. A Behavior can be added to a single object or stacked together with other Behaviors to create unique effects.

Student Activity: Add a Behavior to a Callout

1. Open **BehaveMe.tscproj** from the **Camtasia9Data** Projects folder.

   The BehaveMe project is similar to the AnnotateMe project you closed a few moments ago except it has some additional Callouts added to Tracks 2 and 3. In particular, notice the three ampersands (**&**) added to Track 2 at 6;05, 11;05, and 16;05.

   The stacking order is important. Notice that each ampersand is **behind** the Callouts you added earlier. The stacking effect was easily attained by placing the ampersand in a lower track. In the image above, the **DELETE RESTORE** Callout is in Track 3; the ampersand is in Track 2. Objects in higher tracks are positioned above objects in lower tracks. In the next step, you'll be adding a Behavior to the ampersands.

2. Add a Behavior to a Callout.

   ☐ on Track 2, double-click the **ampersand** positioned at **6;05** to highlight it on the Canvas

   ☐ from the list of tools at the left, click **Behaviors**

   ☐ right-click **Jump And Fall** and choose **Add to selected Media**

The Jump and Fall effect is added to the Callout and appears below the Timeline object. It can be removed by right-clicking and choosing Delete.

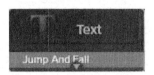

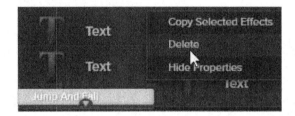

3. Preview the effect.

❏ with the Playhead positioned just to the left of the **ampersand** you just altered, click the **Play** button on the Canvas

The ampersand drops in from the top of the canvas, bounces a few times, and then drops off the bottom of the Canvas.

4. Change the effect's timing.

❏ on the **Timeline**, drag the **left edge** of the **ampersand** Callout **right** a few seconds

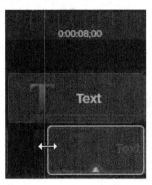

5. Preview the timing change.

   ❑ with the Playhead positioned just to the left of the **RENAME FOLDERS** Callout (the second Callout on Track 2), click the **Play** button on the Canvas

   This time the Callout appears and then, a few seconds later, the animated ampersand does its thing.

6. Modify the effect.

   ❑ on Track 2, double-click the **ampersand** you've been working with to highlight it on the Canvas

   Currently, the ampersand drops in from the top of the Canvas. Let's see what other tricks you can make the Callout perform.

   ❑ on the **Properties** panel, select the **In** tab
   ❑ from the **Style** drop-down menu, choose **Hinge**

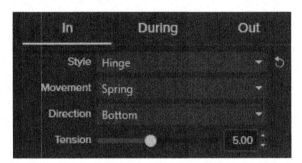

7. Preview the effect.

   ❑ with the Playhead positioned just to the left of the **ampersand** you just altered, click the **Play** button on the Canvas

   This time the ampersand swings up from the bottom of the Canvas.

Behaviors Confidence Check

1. Spend a few moments playing with the **In**, **During**, and **Out** settings available on the **Properties** panel.

2. Add a Behavior to the remaining two ampersands (remember, there are ampersands at Timeline positions 11;05 and 16;05).

3. Preview the effects and adjust the timing of the ampersand Callouts as you see fit.

4. Using the Properties panel, adjust the effects as you see fit.

5. Select and then group mainart image and the Callouts (name the group **Introduction to folders**).

6. Save your work.

Transitions

You can use Transitions to add a smooth, professional visual break between clips in a project. There are several Transition types available on the Transitions panel, including Glow, Fold, and, my personal favorite, Cube rotate.

Student Activity: Add a Transition to a Group

1. Open **TransitionMe.tscproj** from the **Camtasia9Data** Projects folder.

   This project picks up where you left off during the last Confidence Check except I've added a few more grouped assets to the Timeline (Get Ready and Lesson 1).

2. Preview a few Transitions.

   ❑ from the panel at the left, click **Transitions**

   ❑ from the list of **Transitions**, hover above **Glow**

   A sample of the Glow Transition appears on the transition.

   ❑ on the **Transitions** panel, hover above the **Wheel** Transition to see a preview

   ❑ on the Transitions panel, hover above the **Cube rotate** Transition to see a preview

3. Add a Transition to selected media.

   ❑ on the **Timeline**, select the **Get Ready** group

   ❑ on the **Transitions** panel, right-click the **Cube rotate** Transition and choose **Add to Selected Media**

   On the Timeline, a transition has been added to the beginning of the selected group... and it's been added to the beginning of the next group. You can tell that a transition has been added via the green rectangles. The transition was added to the second group (even though you didn't select that group) because, by default, transitions are added to the beginning and end of a selected group and to the beginning of the next group that it is touching.

4. Save your work.

Student Activity: Modify Transition Timing

1. Ensure that the **TransitionMe.tscproj** project is open.

2. Preview the video from the beginning.

   ☐ on your keyboard, press [**ctrl**] [**shift**] [**spacebar**]

   As the video plays on the Canvas, the Cube rotate transition should appear at the beginning and end of the first clip and again at the beginning of the second clip. It's a cool effect, but you'd like to speed it up a bit.

3. Modify Transition Timing.

   ☐ on the Timeline, drag the first green transition a bit to the left

   ☐ drag the second green transition a bit to the right

4. Preview the video.

   The timing for each transition should be a bit faster than before.

Transitions Confidence Check

1. Working in the **TransitionMe** project, add any Transition you like to each of the groups.

2. Preview the project to see transitions.

3. During the preview, did you notice that the transition between clips isn't quite as smooth as it could be (it's almost as if a tiny part of the clip plays twice)? Try this little trick: right-click the **second and third** transitions and deselect **Use Trimmed Content in Transition**.

4. Repeat the process for the remaining transitions.

5. Preview the project to see smoother transitions.

   In my experience, I only leave **Use Trimmed Content in Transition** selected if I want part of a video to appear across a transition—something I rarely need.

6. Save your work.

Notes

iCONLOGiC

"Skills and Drills" Learning

Module 5: Audio

In This Module You Will Learn About:

- Importing Audio Media, page 72
- Voice Narration, page 76
- Splitting Media, page 80
- Audio Editing, page 84

And You Will Learn To:

- Add Background Music to a Video, page 72
- Fade Audio In and Out, page 74
- Record Voice Narration, page 77
- Split a Music Clip, page 80
- Rename Tracks, page 84
- Silence and Cut Audio, page 85

Importing Audio Media

When you import audio media into a Camtasia project, the following formats can be imported: WAV, MP3, M4A, and WMA.

WAV (WAVE): WAV files are one of the original digital audio standards. These kinds of files, while of extremely high quality, can be very large. In fact, typical WAV audio files can easily take up to several megabytes of storage per minute of playing time. If you have a slow Internet connection, download times for files that large are unacceptable.

MP3 (MPEG Audio Layer III): MP3 files are compressed digital audio files. File sizes in this format are typically 90 percent smaller than WAV files.

M4A: M4A (MPEG 4 Audio): M4A files are similar to MP3 files. They are smaller than WAV files but of excellent quality and could one day replace MP3s.

WMA (Windows Media Audio): WMA is a popular audio format developed by Microsoft. WMA files are often smaller than MP3 files.

Student Activity: Add Background Music to a Video

1. Open **AudioMe.tscproj** from the **Camtasia9Data** Projects folder.

2. Add an audio file to the Media Bin.

   ☐ choose **File > Import > Media**

   ☐ navigate to the **Audio_Files** folder within the **Camtasia9Data** folder

   ☐ open **2Step1.mp3**

   The imported audio clip appears in the Media Bin.

3. Add the imported audio to Track 2.

   ☐ on the Media Bin, right-click **2Step1.mp3** and choose **Add to Timeline at Playhead**

   The audio file appears on the Timeline in Track 2 as a series of sharp lines—a waveform.

Audio Confidence Check

1. Still working in the **AudioMe** project, preview the video to hear the background audio you just added to the Timeline.

   Notice that the music lasts longer than the video.

2. On the Timeline, **Track 2**, drag the right edge of the 2Step1.mp3 audio clip left until the audio ends when the video ends at 59;02 seconds.

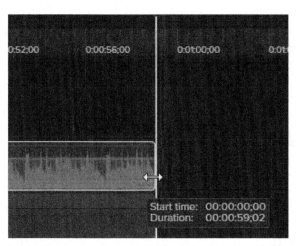

3. Preview the video again. The audio ends when the video ends. However, the audio cuts off a bit too abruptly. You will take care of that next when you learn to fade specific areas of the background music in and out.

Student Activity: Fade Audio In and Out

1. Ensure that the **AudioMe** project is open.

2. Fade audio in.

   ☐ from the panel at the left, click **Audio Effects**

   ☐ on the **Timeline**, select the background music on Track 2

   ☐ from the Audio Effects panel, right-click **Fade In** and choose **Add to Selected Media**

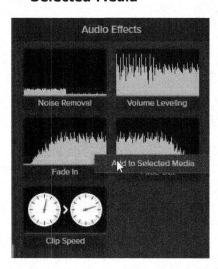

Notice that a ramp has been added to the left of the waveform.

The ramp begins at the bottom of the waveform and then gets taller until the audio hits a consistent level. You can manually drag the green line to control how the audio fades in, but you'll probably be happy with the level established automatically by Camtasia.

3. Fade audio out.

   ☐ on the **Timeline**, ensure that the background music is selected

   ☐ from the **Audio Effects** panel, right-click **Fade out** and choose **Add to Selected Media**

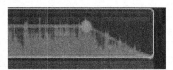

4. Preview the entire video to hear the fade effects you have added to the audio.

Fading Confidence Check

1. Ensure that the **AudioMe** project is open.

2. At the left of Track 2, drag the large dot toward the right a bit to increase the amount of time the Fade In will be in effect.

3. Preview the beginning of the video. You should hear that the Fade In effect lasts longer than before.

4. Go to the end of the Timeline and drag the dot left to increase the amount of time the Fade Out will be in effect.

5. Preview the end of the video. You should hear that the Fade Out effect lasts longer than before.

6. Spend a few moments experimenting with the audio fade timing until the effects sound good to you.

7. At the upper left of the Camtasia window, click **Media**.

8. Select the **Library** panel.

9. Open the **Music Tracks** group and double-click some of the tracks to hear a preview.

10. When you find a track you like, delete the audio you added to Track 2 and replace it with a music track from the Library.

    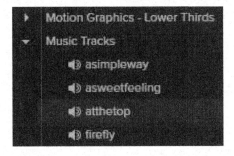

11. Shorten the duration of the music so that it plays only as long as the video.

12. Change the Fade In and Fade Out effects for the music you just added to the Timeline as you see fit.

13. Preview your work.

14. Save your work.

Voice Narration

Camtasia allows you to record your own narration and sound effects and add them to any available Audio Track. If you plan to record your own audio, you will first need a microphone connected to your computer. After the microphone, consider the following:

Voiceover Scripts: You saw an example of an eLearning script on page 22. As with a write a step-by-step eLearning script, it's important to include a voiceover script for yourself or your voiceover talent... and rehearse the script as much as possible prior to recording. Rehearsals are the perfect opportunity to find which words in the script, if any, are going to trip up you or the narrator.

Location, Location, Location: Get yourself into a quiet space—consider a "Do Not Disturb" sign on your door. You might be surprised by how much noise there is in an average office. Your microphone will probably pick up every nearby sound. Before using your office or cubicle as your recording studio, take a break and listen. Turn down the ringer volume on your phone. Is the water dripping? Is the printer squeaking? Is your neighbor coughing nonstop?

USB vs. Analog Microphones: You can use either type of microphone when you record your audio. However, you'll probably get better results using a USB microphone.

Audio Setup: If you plan to use high-end audio hardware, such as a mixer or preamplifier, plug your microphone into the hardware and then plug the hardware into your computer's "line in" port. Set the volume on your mixer or preamplifier to just under zero (this will minimize distortion).

Microphone Placement: The microphone should be positioned four to six inches from your mouth to reduce the chance that nearby sounds will be recorded. Ideally, you should position the microphone above your nose and pointed down at your mouth. Also, if you position the microphone just to the side of your mouth, you can soften the sound of the letters S and P.

Microphone Technique: It's a good idea to keep a glass of water close and, just before recording, take a drink. To eliminate breathing and lip-smack sounds, turn away from the microphone, take a deep breath, exhale, take another deep breath, open your mouth, turn back toward the microphone, and start speaking. Speak slowly. When recording for the first time, many people race through the content. Take your time.

Monitor Your Audio Level As You Record: When recording your audio, you will see an Input Level meter on Camtasia's Voice Narration panel indicating how well the recording process is going. When the meter is green to yellow, you're fine. However, when the meter is orange to red, you are being warned that you are too close to the microphone or that you are speaking too loudly.

Student Activity: Record Voice Narration

1. Using a word processor, open **CreatingFoldersVoiceoverScript** from the **Other_Assets** folder within the Camtasia9Data folder.

   Let's pretend for a moment that you've been hired to serve as the voiceover talent for an eLearning project. It's quite possible you'd get a script similar to the file you've just opened.

   > Audio File 1:
   > Welcome to Super Simplistic Solutions learning series.
   > This is lesson one: Creating New Folders.
   >
   > Audio File 2:
   > This lesson is going to teach you how to create a new folder on your computer, how to rename it, and how to both delete and restore recycled items.
   >
   > Audio File 3:
   > When creating folders keep in mind that you can create as many folders as you need.

2. Rehearse the audio script.

   ☐ using a slow, deliberate cadence, read the following out loud:

   Welcome to Super Simplistic Solutions learning series.

   This is lesson one: Creating New Folders.

   Next you'll record your voice in Camtasia. (You can close the script if you'd like.)

3. Using Camtasia, open **NarrateMe.tscproj** from the **Camtasia9Data** Projects folder.

4. Record voiceover audio.

   ☐ on the **Timeline**, position the Playhead before the **Lesson 1** group

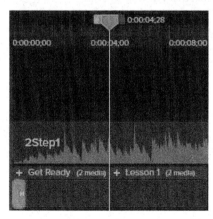

❏ from the panel at the left, click **Voice Narration**

On the Voice Narration panel, notice that I have already pasted the part of the voiceover script you'll be recording. Alternatively, you can print the script and have it beside you during the recording phase.

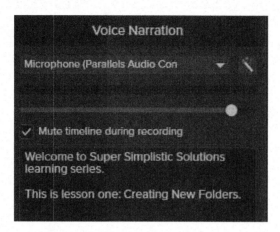

❏ if necessary, select **your microphone** from the drop-down menu

❏ ensure **Mute timeline during recording** is selected

Muting the timeline is a good idea for this video because you have background audio in Track 2. If you don't mute the audio, it will likely play through your computer speakers and ruin your voiceover audio.

And now... prepare yourself! Once you start the recording process, there isn't a count-down or any kind of warning. Instead, Camtasia simply records your voice. While recording, the video will play on the Canvas so you can see what's happening in your lesson while you narrate.

❏ click the **Start Voice Recording** button

❏ using a slow, deliberate cadence, read the following out loud:

Welcome to Super Simplistic Solutions learning series.

This is lesson one: Creating New Folders.

5. When finished, click the **Stop** button.

   The Save Narration As dialog box opens.

   ❐ name the file **My_Lesson1_Voiceover** and save it to the **Audio_Files** folder within the **Camtasia9Data** folder

Once saved, your voiceover narration is automatically added to a new track on the Timeline. In addition, the new audio has been added to the Media Bin.

6. Preview the video.

   You should be able to hear your new voiceover audio. However, you should also be concerned that the audio is hard to understand with the background music playing so loudly. You'll fix that shortly.

7. Save your work.

Splitting Media

You will find Camtasia's ability to split segments on the Timeline to be a valuable feature. Have you imported an audio clip that's too long and difficult to manage? Click at the top of Timeline where you want to split the audio clip and quickly split the clip into as many segments as you need. Want to add a transition in the middle of a video clip? Because transitions cannot be inserted in the middle of a clip, click where you need a transition and insert a split.

Student Activity: Split a Music Clip

1. Open **SplitMe.tscproj** from the **Camtasia9Data** Projects folder.

   This is basically the same project you were just working on except the voiceover audio that you recorded and inserted during the last activity has been replaced by professional voiceover audio.

2. Preview the video.

   Notice that the background music and voiceover audio are fighting with each other. In fact, the background music is so distracting, it's tough to tell what the narrator is saying.

   In the steps that follow, you will split the background music into two parts and then manipulate the two audio pieces on the Timeline so that they don't fight with the voiceover audio. During the splitting process, it's possible not only to split the background music but also to inadvertently split media in other tracks. To prevent that you'll need to lock the tracks. To that end, you will lock both tracks 3 and 1. Changes you make to the media in Track 2 (which will remain unlocked) will not accidentally affect media in other tracks.

   When I first learned how to use Camtasia, there were no books to buy and there was little professional training available. Because I am self-taught on how to use the tool, I was never educated about the need to lock certain tracks before editing objects on other tracks. If I highlighted part of a track and deleted a selection, the same selection in unlocked tracks would also be deleted! In one project, I learned my mistake only hours later when previewing the finished video. By then, it was far too late to undo my mistake.

3. Lock Tracks.

   ❑ at the far left of the Timeline, click the padlock to the left of **Track 1** and **Track 3** to **lock** those tracks (only **Track 2** should remain unlocked)

4. Split the background music in Track 2 into two segments.

   ❏ on the top of the Timeline, click at the **4;29** mark to position the Playhead

   ❏ on the Timeline, select the audio in **Track 2**

   ❏ right-click the **Playhead** and choose **Split**

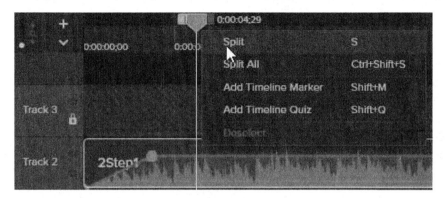

And just like that, the background music has been split into two segments.

Audio Timing Confidence Check

1. Select the second segment of the background music.

2. Drag the **left edge** of the segment to the right until it lines up with the end of the **audio_file01** media in **Track 3**.

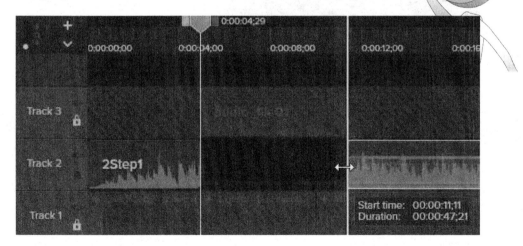

3. Select the **first segment of the background music** and, using the **Audio Effects** panel, **Fade Out** the media.

4. Select the second segment of the background music and **Fade In** the media.

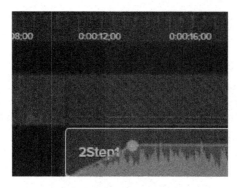

5. Preview the video.

The background music stops pretty much when the narrator begins to speak. Nice. The music shouldn't start again until after the narrator is finished speaking.

There's a problem now with the timing for Lesson 1 group. The group isn't on the Canvas long enough to match the voiceover audio. To fix that, you'll need to change the timing of a few Timeline objects.

6. On the Timeline, unlock both locked tracks.

7. Select and drag both the **Introduction to Folders** and **Creating Folders** groups right by a few seconds (leaving room to stretch the Lesson 1 group).

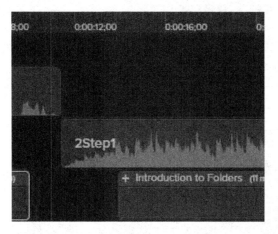

8. Stretch the Lesson 1 group right to make its playtime match the voiceover audio in Track 3.

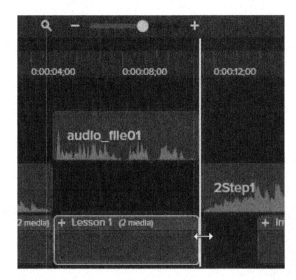

9. Move the Timeline groups as necessary to ensure your Timeline matches the images below.

10. Save your work.

Audio Editing

Earlier in this module you learned how to edit an audio clip by fading the volume in and out. Camtasia offers you other editing options such as the ability to cut segments of a waveform and even replace unwanted audio with silence.

Student Activity: Rename Tracks

1. Open **EditMyAudio.tscproj** from the **Camtasia9Data** Projects folder.

   This project is similar to the project you were just working on with a few notable exceptions. First, two of the tracks have names that are more descriptive than Track 1, Track 2, etc. (Voiceover and Background Audio).

   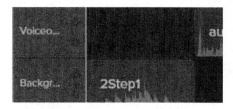

   There's additional voiceover audio in the Voiceover track. And there are additional groups on the Timeline (Introduction to Folders and Folder Specifics).

   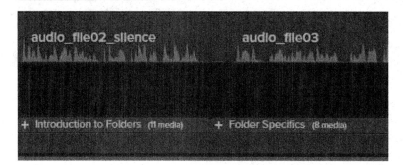

2. Rename a track.

   ❑ on the far left of the Timeline, double-click the name **Track 1**

   ❑ replace the text with the word **Main** and press [**enter**]

   Naming your tracks is always optional. However, in larger project with more than just a few tracks, I find this practice makes it easier and more efficient to produce my projects.

Student Activity: Silence and Cut Audio

1. Ensure that the **EditMyAudio** project is open.

2. Preview an audio clip.

   ❑ on the **Media Bin**, double-click **audio_file02_silence** to preview the clip

   There are two strange sounds in the clip and there's a bit of dead air at the end of the audio file. You have two choices for removing unwanted audio segments: delete the content or replace the content with **Silence**. When deleting, the duration of the audio clip is reduced by the amount of audio that is deleted. However, if your goal is to simply remove a problem in the audio clip (such as click sounds) without altering the duration of the clip, using Silence is an ideal solution.

   ❑ close the Preview window

3. Replace a selection of audio with Silence.

   ❑ lock the **Background** and **Main** tracks

   As you learned earlier, locking a track ensures changes made to other unlocked tracks will not effect locked tracks.

   ❑ on the **Voiceover** track, double-click **audio_file02_silence** to position the Playhead at the beginning of the audio file
   ❑ at the top of the **Timeline**, drag the **Zoom** slider right to zoom closer to the Timeline

   At this enhanced view, you can get a better look at the waveform that makes up the audio file. You can see that the narrator's audio levels are consistent across the wave.

Take a look at about the **15 second** mark on the Timeline. There's a spike in the wave that isn't consistent with the rest of the wave. This part of the wave is an erroneous sound that you need to edit.

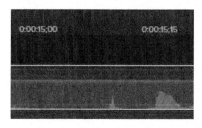

❏ drag the Playhead to the beginning of the errant sound

❏ drag the Playhead's red out point right to highlight the sound

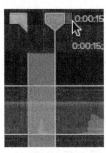

❏ right-click the selection and choose **Silence Audio**

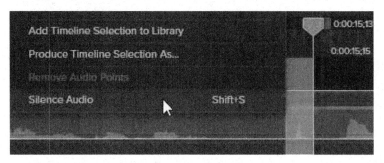

The click sound or whatever it was has been removed without altering the playtime of the media.

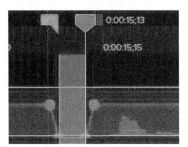

❏ double-click the Playhead to pull the red portion back to its default position (the red box at the right of the Playhead should snap back to the Playhead)

4. Cut audio.

❐ on the Timeline, scroll **right** to the end of the **audio_file02_silence** media

There is a bit of dead air in the audio_file02_silence media that you can delete.

❐ position the Playhead to the left of the last second or so of the **audio_file02_silence** media

❐ drag the Playhead's red out point **right** to select through the end of the media

❐ right-click the selection and choose **Delete**

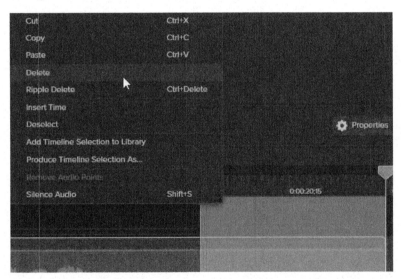

The selected portion of the audio clip is removed leaving a gap on the Timeline. Because the other tracks were locked, the media on those tracks have not been affected.

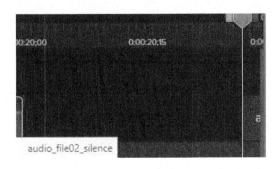

Audio Editing Confidence Check

1. There's another errant sound at about the 16 second mark on the Timeline.

2. Select and then replace the sound with Silence.

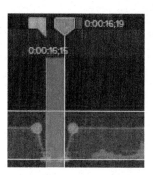

   Note: Remember to double-click the Playhead to return it to its default setting (the red box should snap back to the Playhead).

3. Zoom away from the Timeline far enough so that you can see the gap left on the Timeline when you deleted a portion of the audio media.

4. Drag **audio_file_03 left** to occupy the gap.

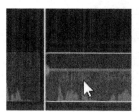

5. Preview the project from the beginning.

   As mentioned earlier, additional media have been added to the project for you. While I've added the media to save you the trouble of doing it yourself (that sounds like a lot of work to me), rest assured that you have learned how to add everything you see during previous lessons.

6. Save your work.

Module 6: Sharing

In This Module You Will Learn About:

- Sharing Videos, page 90
- The Smart Player, page 96
- Watermarks, page 99

And You Will Learn To:

- Share an MP4, page 90
- Share to YouTube, page 94
- Share with a Smart Player, page 97
- Add a Watermark to a Shared Lesson, page 99

Sharing Videos

As you have moved through the first several modules in this book, you learned how to record a video using the Recorder (page 31). Then, beginning on page 42, you learned how to add video to the Editor. Then you added images (page 48), Annotations (page 60), Behaviors (page 65), and audio (page 71). At some point you are going to want to wrap up the development process and produce (publish) your project into a format that your learners can use. Keep in mind that to view your published content, learners will **not** need Camtasia. Instead, learners are able to view your output (assuming they have access to it) using free tools such as Web browsers or media players that are typically found on their computer out of the box.

Camtasia's **Share** menu contains myriad menu items that allow you to quickly publish a project as a standalone file that you can email to a colleague or customer. The standalone file can be opened by free players such as Windows Media Player. You can Share a project so it can be accessed from your internal servers or Learning Management System. Your content can be used by learners on devices such as desktop computers, laptops, and mobile devices (smart-phones, tablets, etc.). There are even Share options allowing you to render and then automatically upload your content to Screencast.com, YouTube, Vimeo, or Google Drive (assuming you have existing accounts with those websites).

Student Activity: Share an MP4

1. Open **ShareMe.tscproj** from the **Camtasia9Data** Projects folder.

2. Produce the video for the web.

   ❏ choose **Share > Local File**

   The Production Wizard opens.

   ❏ select **MP4 only (up to 1080p)** from the drop-down menu

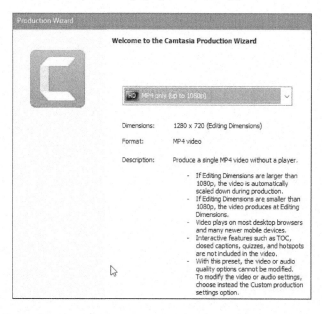

   ❏ click the **Next** button

   The **Where would you like to save your video files(s)?** screen appears.

3. Select a file name and folder.

   ❏ change the **Production name** to **ShareMe_MP4_Only**

   ❏ click the **yellow folder** at the right of the Folder drop-down menu and open the **Produced_Videos** folder (the folder is inside **Camtasia9Data** folder)

   ❏ click the **Save** button

   You should be back in the **Where would you like to save your video files(s)?** window.

   ❏ ensure the remaining options match the picture below

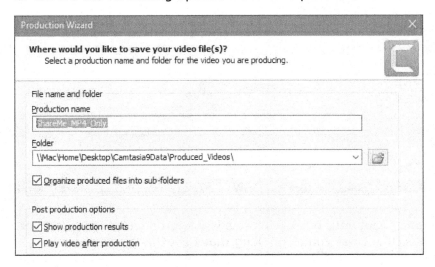

By selecting **Organize produced files into sub-folders** you ensure that the rendered video and its support files are kept together. (Although the video you just produced is a standalone video and does not require support files, other formats that you produce will require several support files.) The two **Post production options**, which you also left selected, show a report of the production process in case there were errors and ensure that your rendered video plays automatically once the rendering process is complete.

4. Render the video.

   ❏ click the **Finish** button

   Your project is rendered. You can track the process on the Rendering Project screen. Generally speaking, the longer your video and the more audio clips you used on the Timeline, the longer the rendering process takes to complete.

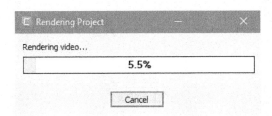

Once the rendering process is complete, the video automatically opens in your default video player and begins to play. In the image below, the video is open in my Windows Media Player.

I don't know about you, but I think this whole production process went just a bit too smoothly. I bet you're thinking that I set this project up in advance so that when you produced it things would go perfectly. And I'm betting that you're betting that once you try to do this on your own, the wheel's going to come off the cart, and nothing is going to work as smoothly as it just did.

Let me assure you that the production process you just worked through was based on default settings you'll find in Camtasia "out of the box." There was nothing in the ShareMe video set up in advance to ensure success in the production process. In fact, you can run through the production process using any Camtasia project, and your result should match those shown in this activity.

You will get a chance to play with some custom Production settings in a bit. For now, enjoy your progress. Believe it or not, you are now a published eLearning author. Congratulations!

5. Review the Production Results.

    ❏ close the media player

    The **Production Results** dialog box contains some important information about your rendered project, including the location of the produced file and the size of the video.

6. View the production files.

    ❏ click the **Open production folder** button

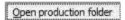

    The **ShareMe_MP4_Only** folder opens. This folder contains the lone rendered file you'll need to deliver to your eLearning customer.

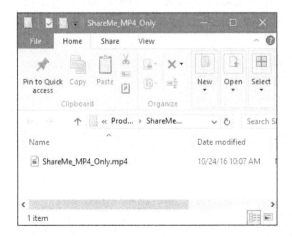

    ❏ close the **ShareMe_MP4_Only** window

    ❏ click the **Finish** button on the Production Results dialog box

Student Activity: Share to YouTube

1. Ensure that the **ShareMe** project should is open.

    Before you can share a video on YouTube, you will need a YouTube account. If you do not already have a YouTube or Gmail account, go to **www.youtube.com** or **gmail.com** now and set one up (it takes only a few moments and is free).

2. Produce a video to be uploaded to YouTube.

    ❏ choose **Share > YouTube**

    The Production Wizard appears again.

    ❏ select **Share to YouTube** from the drop-down menu

    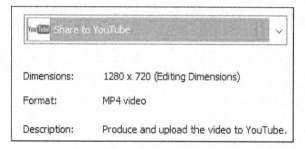

    ❏ click the **Next** button

    You must login to your YouTube account. Once you do, you are taken to the **Produce and Upload to YouTube** screen.

    ❏ click the **Next** button

3. Give the video a Title, Description, and Tags (keywords).

    ❏ in the Title field, type **Creating New Folders**

    ❏ in the Description field, type **This demonstration will teach you how to create a folder using Windows.**

    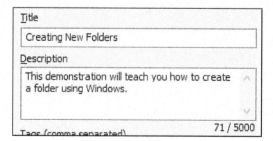

    ❏ in the Tags field, type **training, windows, file management**

    The tags make it easier for YouTube users to search YouTube and find your video.

4. Select a Category.

❑ from the Category drop-down menu, select **Education**

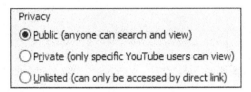

5. Set the Privacy level.

❑ from the Privacy area, select a **Privacy** setting

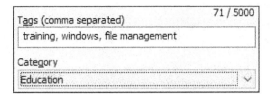

6. Render the video.

❑ click the **Finish** button

The video is rendered again. However, once rendered, it is automatically posted to YouTube.

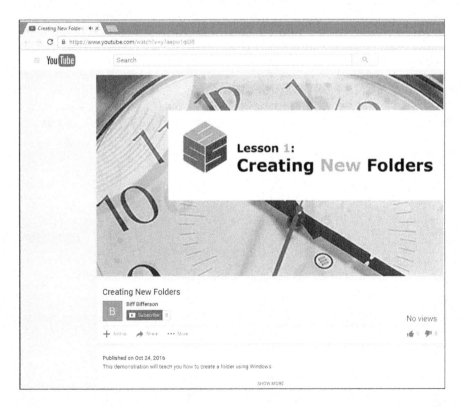

The Smart Player

As you have already seen, producing in Camtasia takes your source content and outputs it into a format that can be consumed (viewed) by the learner. So far you have published videos that play in a media player (MP4) and on YouTube.

When sharing your content using either MP4 or YouTube, it's likely that you saw but did not take the time to read the Description shown below.

Description:	Produce a single MP4 video without a player.
	- If Editing Dimensions are larger than 1080p, the video is automatically scaled down during production. - If Editing Dimensions are smaller than 1080p, the video produces at Editing Dimensions. - Video plays on most desktop browsers and many newer mobile devices. - Interactive features such as TOC, closed captions, quizzes, and hotspots are not included in the video. - With this preset, the video or audio quality options cannot be modified. To modify the video or audio settings, choose instead the Custom production settings option.

The text that gets my attention is the part about interactive features such as TOC, closed captions, and quizzes not being included in the output. Your current project doesn't contain any of that stuff so I wouldn't blame you for moving right past the warning. However, you are soon going to learn how to add interactive content to your project along with closed captions. At that point, MP4 and YouTube sharing isn't going to be an option for you.

If you share a project as **MP4 with Smart Player**, interactive content within your eLearning remains interactive when learners use a browser to access your content from a web server or Learning Management System, even if learners access the content with a mobile device.

Student Activity: Share with a Smart Player

1. Ensure that the **ShareMe** project is open.

2. Produce a video for the web that includes the Smart Player.

   ❏ choose **Share > Local File**

   The Production Wizard appears again.

   ❏ from the drop-down menu, **MP4 with Smart Player (up to 1080p)**

   ❏ click the **Next** button

   ❏ name the Production file **ShareMe_SmartPlayer**

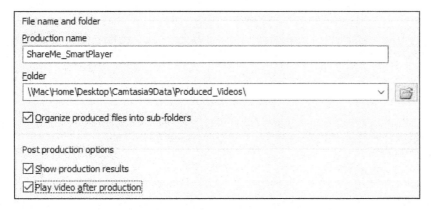

   ❏ click the **Finish** button

   Once rendered, the lesson does not open in the Media Player like last time. This time it opens in your default Web browser.

   ❏ click the **Play** button in the middle of the screen to play the lesson

   The Smart Player appears at the bottom of the window every time you move your mouse within the browser window. The player automatically disappears when you move your mouse away from the browser window.

3. Close the browser window to close the lesson.

4. View the production folder.

☐ from the Production results screen, click the **Open production folder** button

When you published an MP4, the production folder contained only one file (the MP4 video). As you can see, publishing content with the Smart Player results in several output files. Because you're creating content that can play on desktop computers, laptops, and mobile devices, more files are needed to ensure the content remains viable and interactive. All of the files in the output folder are required for the lesson to play on your learner's device.

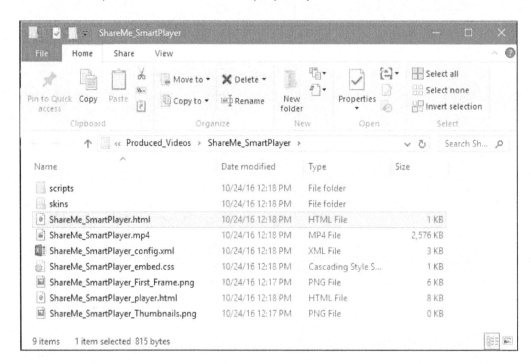

In the image above, I've highlighted one of the output files. The start page is always be the name you typed as you share the content with an html extension added automatically by Camtasia. Although all of the files in this folder are co-dependent and must be uploaded to your server together, the start page is the page your learner's click to get the entire lesson started. If you're working with a webmaster or IT person, he/she needs to know to not only keep the files together but also target the start page with any links that are created for the content you create in Camtasia.

5. Close the production window.

6. Back in Camtasia, close the Production Results screen by clicking the **Finish** button.

Watermarks

Watermarks are ideal if you'd like to add your logo on every slide when the video is produced. You can also use the Watermark feature to add images that denote the video as a "test" or "top secret."

Student Activity: Add a Watermark to a Shared Lesson

1. Ensure that the **ShareMe.tscproj** project is open.

2. Add a watermark.

    ❏ choose **Share > Local File**

    ❏ select **Custom production settings** from the drop-down menu

    ❏ click the **Next** button

    ❏ ensure that **MP4 - Smart Player (HTML5)** is selected

    ❏ click the **Next** button

    Among other things, this second screen allows you to disable the controller (the play bar) if you'd like. You'll leave the default settings.

    ❏ click the **Next** button again

3. Add a watermark.

    ❏ from the Watermark area, select **Include watermark**

    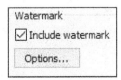

    ❏ click the **Options** button just below Include watermark

The Watermark options appear along with a Watermark Preview window.

☐ click the **Browse** button at the right (the yellow folder)

☐ from the **Camtasia9Data\Image_Files** folder, open **ForReviewOnly**

The image appears, by default, in the lower right of the Watermark Preview.

4. Change the position of the watermark.

☐ from the **Position** area, click the **top right** square (you may need to move the Watermark Preview window out of the way to see the Position area)

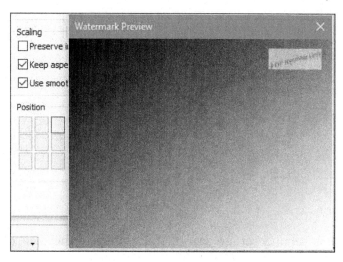

5. Remove a watermark's background color.

☐ from the **Effects** area, select **Use transparent color**

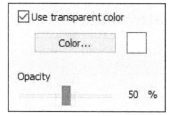

The background color behind the logo has been removed.

6. Change the Image scale.

   ❏ from the **Image scale** area, drag the slider until the scale changes to **30%**

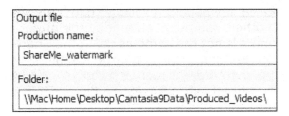

   ❏ click the **OK** button
   ❏ click the **Next** button to move to the final screen

7. Give the video a new production name.

   ❏ change the Production name to **ShareMe_watermark**

Output file
Production name:

ShareMe_watermark

Folder:

\\Mac\Home\Desktop\Camtasia9Data\Produced_Videos\

   ❏ click the **Finish** button

   After rendering, the video (including the watermark), opens in your default web browser.

8. Close the browser.

9. Back in Camtasia, close the Production Results dialog box (click the **Finish** button).

10. Save your work.

Sharing Confidence Check

1. If you have a Vimeo account, Share your project to Vimeo.

2. If you have a Google Drive account, Share your project to your drive. (You should be able to use the same account credentials you used for sharing on YouTube.)

Sharing is the process of taking your final work and rendering a version of the project that can be accessed without the need for the learner to own Camtasia. Shared output files are not the original Camtasia project files so the content cannot be modified by the learner (the learner would need both Camtasia 9, the original Camtasia project, and the media assets to make any changes to your content).

If you work with a team of Camtasia developers it's likely that you will be asked to share your project with others (so they can modify the project). Sharing projects between developers is not the same as using the Share menu so you can render content for your learner. Sharing a project sounds simple enough: copy the **tscproj** file to a shared drive such as Dropbox or a network drive and that's that. However, assets added to the Media Bin are **linked** to their original location. When you import media into Camtasia from a local or network drive and then send the Camtasia project file to someone outside your network, that person is prompted to locate the linked media before the project opens in his/her copy of Camtasia. It's likely that that person will not be able to find those linked assets.

Here's how to get past that problem:

3. Choose **File > Export as Zip**.

4. Click the yellow folder and select a destination on your computer or network. (Ensure **Include all files from Media Bin in zip** is selected.)

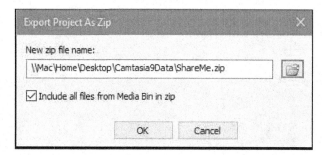

5. Click the **OK** button.

The resulting zip file contains all of your project's assets. You can now share this zip file with fellow Camtasia developers who have everything they need to open and edit the project (assuming they also have Camtasia 9 or newer installed).

Module 7: Extending, Zooming, Trimming, and Interactivity

In This Module You Will Learn About:

- Extending Frames, page 104
- Trimming, page 107
- Zoom-n-Pan, page 109
- Markers, page 112
- TOCs, page 114
- Hotspots, page 117

And You Will Learn To:

- Extend a Video Frame, page 104
- Trim a Video Selection, page 107
- Add a Zoom-n-Pan, page 109
- Add a Marker, page 112
- Add a TOC, page 114
- Add a Hotspot to the Timeline, page 117

Extending Frames

When using the Camtasia Recorder, some people elect to record their voiceover audio while recording the screen. In my experience, recording audio while recording screen actions can work splendidly, but it can also lead to audio that is such a mess that the entire recording needs to be redone. If, however, you record screen actions and then import audio later (as you've done several times during the lessons in this book), synchronizing the screen actions shown in the video with the voiceover audio can be difficult. In those instances where the voiceover audio is referring to something before the event occurs in the video, you'll be happy to learn that you can extend the playtime of a single video frame until the video and the audio catch up to each other.

Student Activity: Extend a Video Frame

1. Open **ExtendZoomMe.tscproj** from the **Camtasia9Data** Projects folder.

2. At the **43;14 second mark** on the Timeline, notice that **audio_file04** has been added to the Timeline above the **Creating Folders** group.

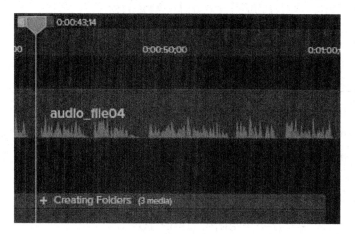

3. Position the Playhead at 43;14 and preview the video.

   In the video, the narrator is talking about how simple and similar the process of creating a folder is on most operating systems. However, he doesn't get to the actual step-by-step process of creating the folder until 56;00. During those first 13 seconds, the mouse is moving around the screen and, besides being distracting, has already shown the process of creating the folder before the narrator gives the step-by-step instructions. You're going to extend the playtime of the first part of the video by 13 seconds to synchronize what the narrator is saying with the video.

4. Disable Playhead Snapping.

   ❐ choose **View > Enable Playhead Snapping** (to **disable** the command)

   Note: A check mark next to a menu item means the item is enabled. Because you'll next be positioning the Playhead at a very specific location, you need to disable Playhead Snapping otherwise it'll be difficult if not impossible to position the Playhead as instructed during the next step. If the instruction above resulted in Enable Playhead Snapping being enabled, perform the step again to ensure it is disabled.

5. Extend a video frame.

❏ on the **Timeline**, zoom a bit closer to the **43** second mark

❏ on the **Timeline**, drag the Playhead to **43;16**

As mentioned above, you disabled Playhead Snapping which allowed you to move the Playhead a tenth of a second from the beginning of the segment. If you had left Playhead Snapping enabled, you would not have been able to position the Playhead so precisely.

❏ open the **Creating Folders** group

❏ right-click the video and choose **Extend Frame**

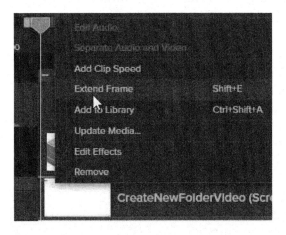

❏ change the Duration to **13.6**

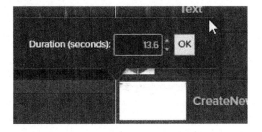

❏ click the **OK** button

Timeline Confidence Check

1. Preview the video from the beginning of the Creating Folders group.

   Although extending the frame has delayed the mouse action on screen, the video is now cut off and ends abruptly.

2. Zoom away from the Timeline.

3. Extend the playtime for the items in the Creating Folders group enough so that the entire video plays.

4. Continue to adjust the timing for the individual objects in the Creating Folders group until the timing is similar to the image below.

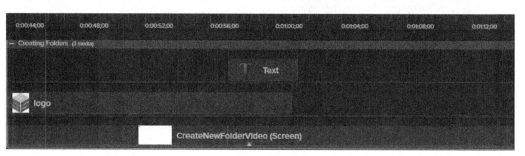

5. Preview the video from the beginning of the Creating Folders group and, if not satisfied with your timing, make any necessary adjustments.

6. Save your work.

Trimming

When using the Camtasia Recorder to record screen actions, there will come a time when you move the mouse the wrong direction or click the wrong thing. In those instances, move your mouse pointer back to its previous location, audibly count down 3, 2,1, and then perform the step correctly. Because it's easy to trim a portion of the recording in the Editor, this technique is more efficient than starting over again.

The video in the Creating Folders group has a bit of a mouse timing issue. At the 1:04;11 mark (assuming you extended the frame timing as instructed earlier in this module), the mouse pointer is supposed to move smoothly from the **Home** tab to the **New Folder** icon. However, the pointer hovers a bit too long over the Paste icon. You're going to trim that small portion of the video.

Student Activity: Trim a Video Selection

1. Ensure that the **ExtendZoomMe.tscproj** is open.

   Note: During the "Extend a Video Frame" activity that begins on page 104 you added **13.6 seconds of playtime** to the video when you extended the frame. Please ensure that you completed that activity and the Confidence Check that followed before moving forward otherwise the timing mentioned below will not match your project.

2. Preview the portion of the video needing to be cut.

   ❑ on the **Timeline**, position the **Playhead** at **1:03;00**

   ❑ use the **Canvas** to preview a few seconds of the video

   As mentioned above, at this point in the video, the mouse pointer does not move smoothly from the **Home** tab to the **New Folder** icon.

3. Select and trim a portion of the video.

   ❑ if necessary, collapse the **Creating Folders** group

   ❑ right-click the **Creating Folders** group and choose **Ungroup**

   ❑ on the **Timeline**, position the **Playhead** at **1:04;13**

   This is the exact point in the video when the mouse pointer hesitates over the Paste icon.

   ❑ drag the **Outpoint** (the red box) a bit to the right to **1:04;27**

❏ right-click the selection and choose **Cut**

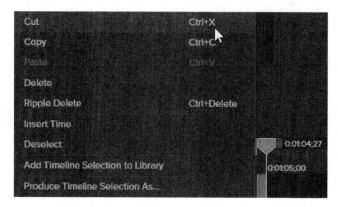

The selected portion of the video is trimmed.

Note: Keep in mind that anything in the tracks above or below the media you just edited were also cut. In this instance, there wasn't anything in those tracks so you're good. Just remember to lock any tracks in your projects that you do not want to edit.

4. Preview changes.

❏ on the Timeline, position the **Playhead** at approximately **1:02;00**

❏ use the Canvas to preview a few seconds of the video

The mouse cursor hesitation has been removed.

5. Re-enable Playhead Snapping. (View menu.)

6. Save your work.

Zoom-n-Pan

The Zoom-n-Pan feature is useful if the width and height of your project are large and you want to focus the learner's attention on a specific area of the screen. Zooming moves the learner closer to the screen; Panning automatically moves the screen for the learner. Adding Zooms and Pans is as simple as positioning the Playhead where you want to add the effect, accessing the Zoom-n-Pan panel (via Animations) and stretching and/or moving the Zoom-n-Pan window.

Student Activity: Add a Zoom-n-Pan

1. Ensure that the **ExtendZoomMe.tscproj** is open.

2. Add a Zoom-n-Pan mark.

   ❏ on the **Timeline**, position the Playhead at **59;22**

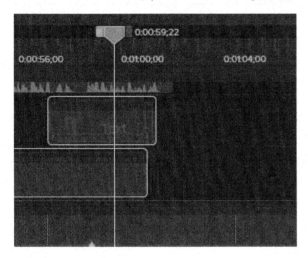

   This is the area of the video where the mouse pointer has arrived at the Home tab and is about to click.

   ❏ from the list of tools at the left, click **Animations**

   There are two options: Zoom-n-Pan and Animations.

   ❏ click **Zoom-n-Pan**

   On the Zoom-n-Pan panel, notice that there is a box around the entire preview. If left alone, there won't be any zoom or pan effect applied to the video because you haven't yet told Camtasia to do anything to the video at the Playhead position.

❏ on the **Zoom-n-Pan** panel, drag the lower right resizing handle **up** and to the **left** similar to the picture below

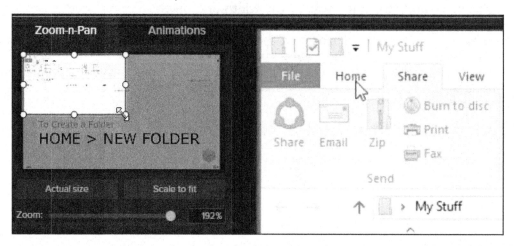

As you drag the resizing handle on the Zoom-n-Pan panel, the effect is automatically added to the video, and you get closer to the Canvas.

On the Timeline, notice that animation markers (arrows with a dot at each end) have been added. On each animation marker, the first dot is the point on the Timeline where the video begins to zoom in; the larger dot is when the zoom is complete. The video then stays at that zoom setting until further notice. You can alter the timing of the zooming action by dragging the dots. And you can view and edit the Properties of the zoom by double-clicking the end dot.

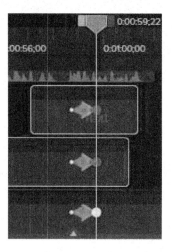

3. Preview the Zoom-n-Pan.

   ❏ on the **Timeline**, position the **Playhead** at the **57;00** mark

   ❏ on the **Canvas**, click the **Play** button

   Notice that, thanks to the Zoom-n-Pan feature, you are automatically taken closer to the action on the screen.

4. Zoom back out.

☐ on the **Timeline**, position the Playhead at approximately the **1:07** mark

At this part of the video, the new folder has been created—a perfect place to zoom back out.

☐ on the **Zoom-n-Pan** panel, drag the lower right resizing handle **down** and to the **right** similar to the picture below

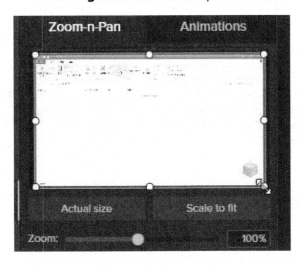

On the Timeline, notice that there is a second set of Zoom-n-Pan markers.

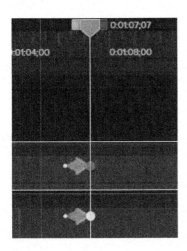

5. Preview the changes.

☐ on the **Timeline**, position the Playhead just to the left of the first Zoom-n-Pan markers

☐ on the Canvas, click the **Play** button

The Zoom-n-Pan should occur twice (once for the zoom in; once for the zoom out). Admit how awesomely cool that really is!

6. Save your work.

Markers

Markers create navigation points within a video. When you add a table of contents (TOC; you will learn about TOCs on page 114) to your finished lesson, the markers you add can be used to create hyperlinks (jumps) throughout the lesson. Allowing your learners to jump around the lesson is known as Branching.

Student Activity: Add a Marker

1. Open **MarkMe_TOCMe.tscproj** from the **Camtasia9Data** Projects folder.

2. Add a Marker.

   Notice that there is a new track in this project: Buttons. This track contains three shapes that learners will be able to click to access specific areas of the course. You'll be adding markers to this area of the project as well as the three specific areas of the course: Creating Folders, Renaming Folders, and Recycling.

   ❑ ensure the **Playhead** is as **far left** on the **Timeline** as it can go

   ❑ choose **Modify > Markers > Add Timeline Marker**

   A marker has been added above the Timeline. In the upper right of the Camtasia window, the new marker is ready to receive a name.

   ❑ at the upper right of the window, change the **Maker name** to **Home**

   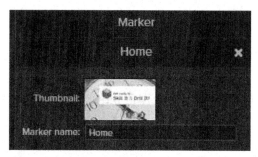

Marking Confidence Check

1. Still working in the MarkMe_TOCMe project, move the Playhead **right** to the **Lesson 1** group.

2. Add a new marker (**Modify > Markers > Add Timeline Marker**) named **Lesson 1: Creating New Folders**.

3. Position the Playhead at the **Lesson 2** group.

4. Add a new marker named **Lesson 2: Renaming Folders**.

5. Position the Playhead at the **Lesson 3** group.

6. Add a new marker named **Lesson 3: Recycling and Restoring**.

   Your project should now contain four markers.

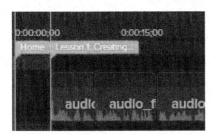

7. Save your work.

TOCs

If you'd like to allow your learners to control the learning experience and navigate (branch) through your lesson in any order they'd like, you can add a TOC to your video during the Production process. To include a TOC in a produced lesson, you first need to add markers to your project (as you learned to do on page 112). When you add the TOC, you can elect to use the marker names as the hyperlinks on your TOC or make up new names "on the fly."

> **Note:** Before attempting to work with a TOC, you must first complete the "Markers" activity that begins on page 112.

Student Activity: Add a TOC

1. Ensure that the **MarkMe_TOCMe** project is open.

2. Share a project using Custom production settings.

    ❏ choose **Share > Local File** and then select **Custom production settings** from the drop-down menu

    ❏ click the **Next** button

3. Select the output format.

    ❏ if necessary, select **MP4 - Smart Player (HTML5)**

    ❏ click the **Next** button

4. Ensure a Table of Contents is included in the output.

    ❏ on the **Controller** tab, ensure Produce with controller is selected (you cannot include a TOC without a controller)

    ❏ select the **Options** tab

    ❏ ensure that **Table of contents** is selected (this is the default setting)

    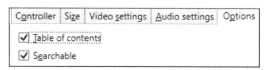

    ❏ click the **Next** button

5. Add a web page title bar.

☐ from the **HTML** area, click the **HTML options** button

☐ change the Title to **Working with Folders**

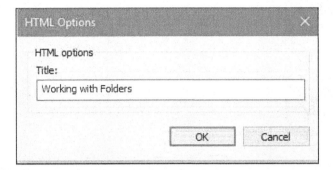

☐ click the **OK** button

☐ click the **Next** button

You should now be at the **Marker options** screen where you can control a few Table of Contents attributes.

☐ from the bottom left of the screen, **Display options** area, ensure **Fixed-left** is selected

☐ from the **Marker display** drop-down menu, choose **Text only**

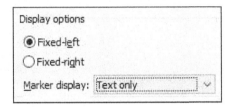

☐ click the **Next** button

☐ click the **Finish** button

Your video is rendered. Depending on the processing power of your computer, the process could take a few minutes to complete. Once rendered, the lesson opens in your default web browser.

6. Watch the finished video.

☐ click the **Play** button to start the video

☐ move your mouse to the bottom of the video to display the Controller

☐ on the **Controller**, click the **TOC** button

Look at that... a TOC appears at the left of the video, and your markers appear, just like magic. You can click any of the markers on the TOC to jump from lesson to lesson.

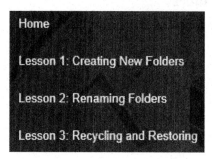

7. Close the browser window.

8. Back in Camtasia, click the **Finish** button and then save your work.

Hotspots

To maximize the effectiveness of your eLearning videos, you can add interactivity via a hotspot. The hotspots you add can allow your learners to jump to specific markers within a video, add hyperlinks to websites, and more.

Here are the options available to you when you create a Hotspot:

Pause at End: Once clicked, the video stops based on the hotspot's end time on the Timeline.

URL: Takes the learner to a website.

Marker: Takes the learner to a specific Timeline marker.

Time: Takes the learner to a specific time in the video.

> **Note:** If you include a Hotspot in your project, you must produce the lesson as **MP4 - Smart Player (HTML5)** for the hotspot to remain a clickable object in the rendered lesson.

Student Activity: Add a Hotspot to the Timeline

1. Open **HotSpotMe.tscproj** from the Camtasia9Data Projects folder.

   As mentioned earlier in this module, there are three shapes at the beginning of the course that learners will be able to click to jump to a specific lesson. You've added the source of those jumps when you added the Creating Folders, Renaming Folders, and Recycling markers earlier.

2. Add an Interactive Hotspot to the project.

   ❏ on the **Timeline**, ensure that the **Playhead** is as **far left** as it can go

   ❏ from the list of tools at the left, click **Annotations**

   ❏ click **Special**

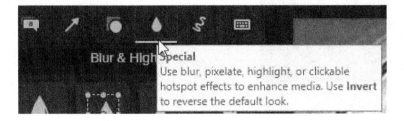

☐ right-click **Interactive Hotspot** and choose **Add to Timeline at Playhead**

The hotspot is added to the middle of the Canvas.

☐ on the Canvas, position and resize the hotspot over the red shape similar to the image below

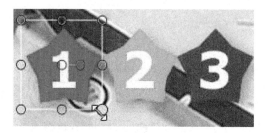

3. Add an Action to a Hotspot.

☐ with the hotspot selected, go to the **Properties** panel

☐ from the Interactive Hotspot area, ensure **Pause at End** is selected (this ensures that the video doesn't move forward without giving the learner a chance to click)

☐ select **Marker**

☐ from the drop-down menu, choose **Lesson 1: Creating New Folders** (you learned how to create markers on page 112)

4. Save your work.

Hotspot Confidence Check

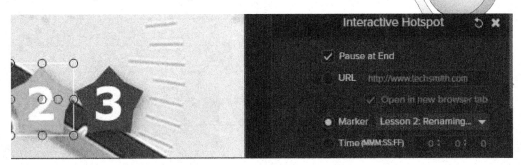

1. Add a second Interactive Hotspot and position it over the red shape.

2. Make the target of the hotspot the Lesson 2 marker.

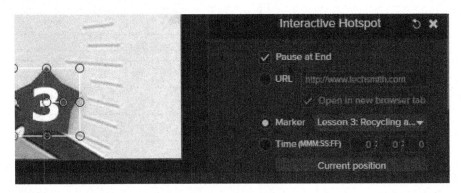

3. Add a third Interactive Hotspot and position it over the black shape.

4. Make the target of the hotspot the Lesson 3 marker.

5. Share the project as **MP4 with Smart Player**.

6. Once the video is rendered, test the hotspots in your web browser.

7. When finished, close all browser windows and, back in Camtasia, close the Production Results dialog box.

8. Save your work.

Notes

Module 8: Quizzes and Screencast.com

In This Module You Will Learn About:

- Quizzes, page 122
- Screencast.com, page 129

And You Will Learn To:

- Add a Quiz and Multiple Choice Question, page 122
- Add a Fill In the Blank Question, page 126
- Share to Screencast.com, page 129

Quizzes

I have never been a very good test-taker. The minute I hear a course I am taking includes a quiz, I fixate on the pending quiz or exam and get myself so stressed out that I stop learning.

It's only recently that I've come to understand quizzes and exams for what they are... an opportunity to learn. Had I thought of quizzes as just another part of the learning process, perhaps I wouldn't have stressed myself out so much and would have performed better on tests (there have been many poor performances over the years).

Many people compare eLearning to live training. It's not a fair comparison because eLearning lacks live, human interaction. In a live, instructor-led class, an experienced trainer can gauge the effectiveness of a lesson by asking the learner a question about something taught in the class. When a trainer asks questions, the learner has an opportunity to share what was learned, and prove lesson comprehension. It's perfectly fine for the learner in a live class to get a question wrong. In that instance, the trainer gives the correct answer and learning has taken place. In my classes, I typically ask direct and overhead questions of my students. If the answer given is wrong, I give the correct answer. Later, I'll ask that same learner the question again... only I reword the question (I'm sneaky like that). In almost every instance, the learner answers the rephrased question correctly.

Although an eLearning lesson cannot provide trainer-to-learner interaction, you can still engage the learner by adding a quiz to a Camtasia project. Each quiz can contain any or all of the following question types: Multiple choice, True/False, Fill in the blank, and Short answer.

> **Note:** If you intend to include a quiz in your eLearning lesson, you must produce the video using MP4 - Smart Player or the quiz will not work.

Student Activity: Add a Quiz and Multiple Choice Question

1. Open **QuizMe.tscproj** from the Camtasia9Data Projects folder.

2. Position the Playhead where you'd like the quiz to appear.

   ❏ on the **Timeline**, position the **Playhead** at **3:11;26**

3. Insert a quiz.

   ❏ from the list of tools at the left, click **Interactivity**

   The Quizzing panel opens at the top left of the Editor.

   ❏ click **Add Quiz to Timeline**

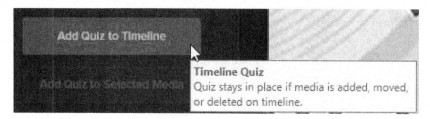

The new quiz is created. Using the options on the Quiz properties (in the upper right of the Camtasia window), you can name the quiz, add questions, preview the quiz, and more.

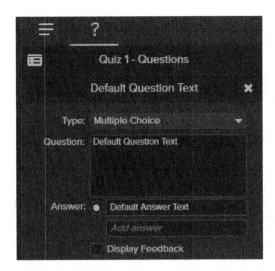

The quiz also appears on the Timeline with a default name, Quiz 1.

4. Rename the quiz.

   ☐ on the Quiz Properties panel, click **Quiz Options**

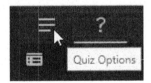

   ☐ change the Quiz Name to **Folders Quiz**

5. Ensure that the quiz will score.

   ☐ from just above the **Preview** button, ensure both **Score quiz** and **Viewer can see their results** are selected

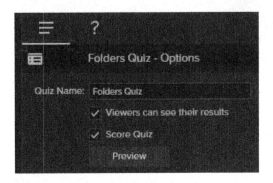

6. Specify the question type.

   ☐ on the **Quiz Properties** panel, click **Quiz Question Properties**

   ☐ from the **Type** drop-down menu, ensure **Multiple Choice** is selected

7. Edit the question.

   ☐ in the Question area, replace the placeholder text with **When giving a folder a name, how many characters can you use?**

8. Add four answers to the question.

   ☐ in the first Answer area, type **9**

   ☐ in the next Answer area, type **255**

   ☐ in the next Answer area, type **11**

   ☐ in the next Answer area, type **218**

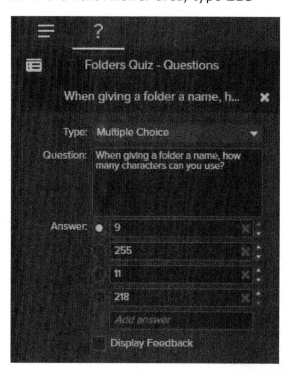

Note: You'll always end up with an extra "Add answer..." placeholder (as shown in the image above). No worries. Unless you type something in that placeholder, the answer will not be part of the quiz.

9. Specify 255 as the correct answer.

   ❏ click the circle next to the second answer, 255

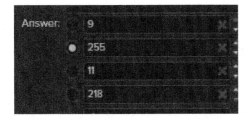

10. Save your work.

Student Activity: Add a Fill In the Blank Question

1. Ensure that the **QuizMe** project is open.

2. Add a question.

   ☐ from the bottom of the Quiz properties panel, click **Add question**

   The new question appears below the first.

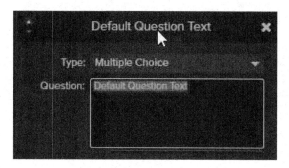

3. Specify the question type.

   ☐ from the **Type** drop-down menu, choose **Fill in the Blank**

4. Edit the question.

   ☐ replace the Question Text placeholder text with **The New Folder icon is found on the _____ tab of the Ribbon.**

5. Edit the Answer.

   ☐ in the **Answer** area, replace the placeholder text with **Home**

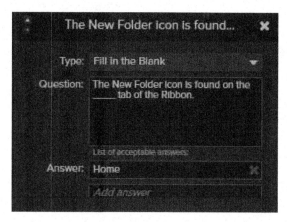

6. Save your work.

Quiz Confidence Check

1. Preview the quiz by clicking **See how Quiz looks in your viewer**.

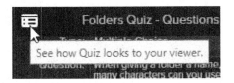

A preview of the quiz appears on the Canvas.

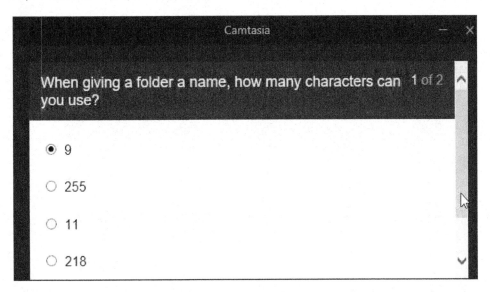

2. Select any of the answers in the first question and click the **Next** button (you'll likely need to scroll down to see the Next button).

3. Type anything you'd like into the text field within the **Fill in the Blank** question and then click the **Submit Answers** button.

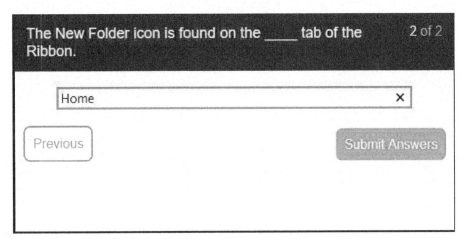

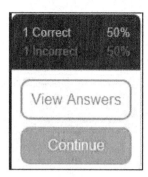

4. Click the **View Answers** button.

Correct answers are shown with a green check mark. Wrong answers are flagged with a red X.

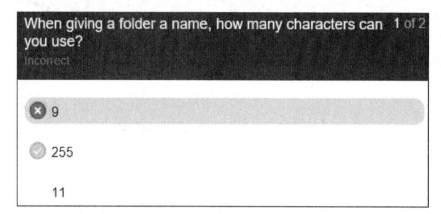

5. Close the Quiz preview.

6. Save the project.

Screencast.com

When you Share your Camtasia project, you can share it to YouTube, Vimeo, etc. However, if you Share the finished project locally, then what? How do your learners gain access to your content? If you have a Learning Management System or web server of your own, you can upload the rendered output files there. But what if you don't have either of those? Where can you upload your content so that it is easily readily available and, if it contains interactivity such as hotspots or a quiz, ensure that the interactivity works? Fortunately, TechSmith provides a free service called Screencast where you can test and share your content. The video you are about to work with contains a quiz. You'll upload the video to Screencast.com and be able to test the quiz.

> **Note:** You will need to create a free account on Screencast.com prior to starting the activity below. If you do not have an account, go to **www.screencast.com** and set one up now.

Student Activity: Share to Screencast.com

1. Open **ScreencastMe.tscproj** from the Camtasia9Data Projects folder.

2. Produce and share a video on Screencast.com.

   ❏ choose **Share > Screencast.com**

   ❏ enter your Screencast.com email address and password

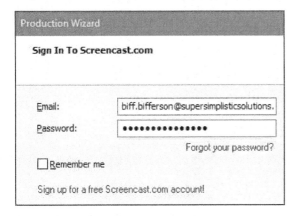

   ❏ click the **Next** button

   ❏ click the **Next** button to leave the Video title as is

3. Set up the Quiz Reporting Options.

   ❏ select **Report quiz results through email**

   ❏ in the Recipient email address and Confirm email address fields, type **your email address**

4. Require Viewer identity.

   ❏ from the **Viewer identity** area, select **Require viewers to input name & email address**

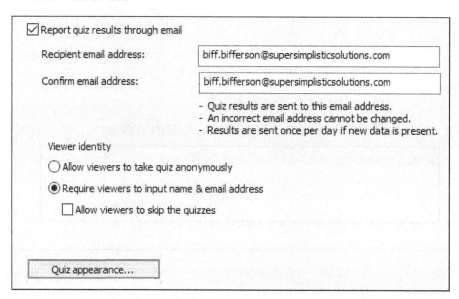

   ❏ click the **Finish** button

The lesson is produced and then automatically uploaded into your Screencast account.

Screencast Confidence Check

1. Switch to your web browser. You should already be logged into Screencast.com. If so, move to the next step. If you are not logged into Screencast.com, use a web browser to access Screencast.com and login. Once logged in, your uploaded video automatically opens.

2. Start the video and you will be prompted to identify yourself (thanks to the **Viewer identity** option you selected a moment ago).

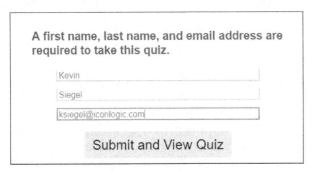

3. Fill in the fields with your first name, last name, and email address.

4. Click the **Submit and View Quiz** button.

5. When the time comes to take the quiz, take it. You can answer the questions correctly or incorrectly.

6. After taking the quiz, continue through to the end of the video. When finished, close the browser.

7. If you have access to email, check you email. The quiz results should be sent to you from Camtasia Quiz Service. The email comes from services@techsmith.com. If you don't see the email, you might want to check your SPAM folder and/or add TechSmith to your server's White List. Also, it was several hours before I received my first email from TechSmith.

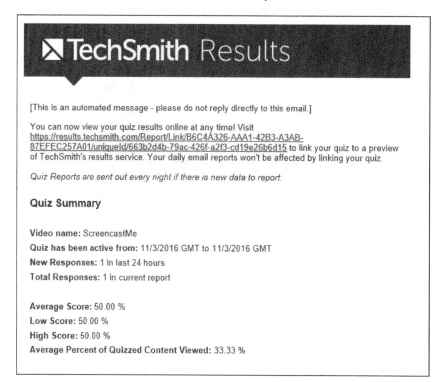

The Quiz results include a summary containing the number of responses, the average score, the low score, and the high score. Specific details about the quiz results are included as CSV files that can be opened with Microsoft Excel or other spreadsheet applications. The CSV files contain details about who took the quiz, the questions they got right and wrong, etc.

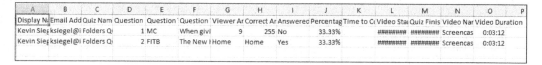

8. Close the e-mail (there is no need to save or send the e-mail).

9. Back in Camtasia, close any open dialog boxes and save your work.

Module 9: PowerPoint and Captions

In This Module You Will Learn About:

- PowerPoint to Camtasia, page 134
- Captions, page 137

And You Will Learn To:

- Record PowerPoint, page 134
- Manually Create Closed Captions, page 137
- Control Caption Timing, page 141
- Use Speech-to-Text to Create Closed Captions, page 144

PowerPoint to Camtasia

You wouldn't think that a Microsoft product (PowerPoint) would have anything to do with a TechSmith product (Camtasia). However, I frequently meet Subject Matter Experts who have created perfectly good PowerPoint presentations. Unfortunately, PowerPoint does not have the ability to add quizzes or automatically upload content to YouTube or Screencast.com. Rather than try to recreate the PowerPoint presentation within Camtasia, you can record the PowerPoint presentation using Camtasia and create eLearning from existing PowerPoint content.

Student Activity: Record PowerPoint

1. If Camtasia is running, close the program.

2. Open a PowerPoint presentation with Microsoft PowerPoint.

   ❑ using Microsoft PowerPoint, open **S3_Policies** from the **Camtasia9Data**, **Other_Assets** folder

   The Camtasia PowerPoint Add-in is automatically installed on your computer by the Camtasia application installer. Unless it has been disabled, you should be greeted with the alert dialog box below. (You can also confirm that the Camtasia Add-in has been installed by choosing **File > Options > Add-ins**.)

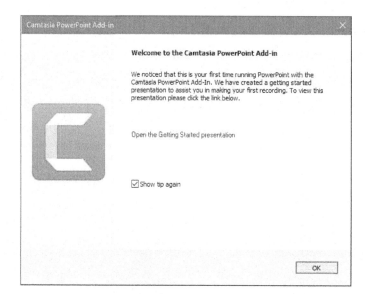

   ❑ click the **OK** button

   ❑ on the **Ribbon**, click the **Add-Ins** tab

   Camtasia recording tools appear in the upper left of the PowerPoint window.

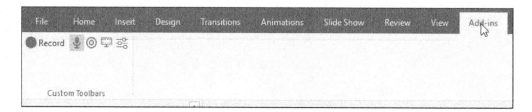

3. Record the PowerPoint presentation.

   ❒ from the Custom Toolbars area, click the **Record** tool

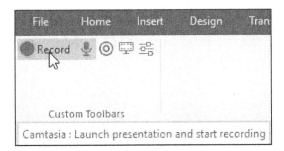

The PowerPoint slide show begins.

   ❒ in the lower right of the slide show, click the **Click to begin recording** button

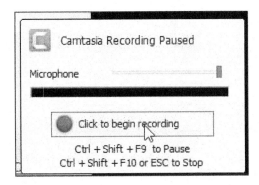

At this point, the presentation is being recorded, much like your screen was recorded when you learned to use Camtasia Recorder (on page 29).

   ❒ take your time and click in the middle of each slide to progress through the slide show

When you reach the end of the slide show, you'll be alerted with a dialog box.

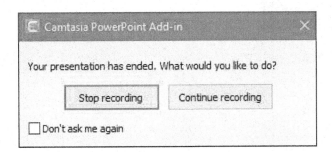

   ❒ click the **Stop Recording** button

Next you will be prompted to save the recording.

   ❒ navigate to **Camtasia9Data** folder
   ❒ open the **Video_Files** folder and then save the file

You will be asked if you'd like to **Produce your recording** or **Edit your recording**. The former will take you directly to the Share options where you can elect to produce the video for Screencast.com, for YouTube, or as HTML5. The latter opens the recording in the Camtasia Editor where you can enhance the video using any of the production techniques you've learned to add during the lessons throughout this book (add annotations, audio, quizzes, behaviors, images, videos, etc.).

❐ select **Edit your recording**

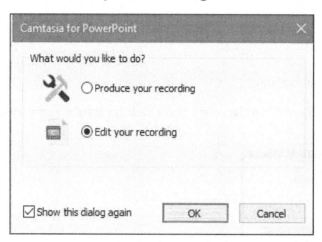

❐ click the **OK** button

And that's that. Your PowerPoint presentation has been added to the Media Bin. At this point, you could move forward and produce, and then Share, the content as you have learned to do throughout this book.

Captions

Closed captioning allows you to provide descriptive information in your published eLearning project that typically matches the voiceover audio contained in your Camtasia project.

There are a couple of ways you can add closed captions to a Camtasia project. The following lessons show you how to add the captions manually (by transcribing), and how to create the Captions automatically via Speech-to-Text.

Student Activity: Manually Create Closed Captions

1. Open **CaptionMe.tscproj** from the **Camtasia9Data** Projects folder.

   If prompted to save the project from the last activity, there is no need to do so.

   There are seven audio clips in the Voiceover track. You're going to listen to the audio, painful if it might sound as if your typing skills aren't the best, and transcribe the audio you hear as closed captions.

2. Add captions manually.

   ☐ from the list of tools at the left, click **Captions** (if your display size is small, you might need to click the **More button** at the bottom of the list of tools and then click **Captions**)

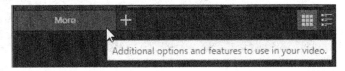

   ☐ on the **Timeline**, position the **Playhead** at exactly 5;00 (this is where the first voiceover audio clip is positioned)

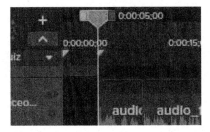

   ☐ on the **Canvas**, click the **Play** button and listen to the audio

   In this first audio segment, the narrator says: "Welcome to Super Simplistic Solutions learning series. This is lesson one: Creating New Folders."

   ☐ on the **Timeline**, re-position the **Playhead** at exactly 5;00

☐ click the **Add Caption** button

A Callout is added to both Track 4 and the Canvas.

☐ on the Canvas, type the following into the space beneath the background image: **Welcome to Super Simplistic Solutions learning series.**

3. Format the Caption text.

☐ click the **Font Properties** drop-down menu and change the **Size** to **24**

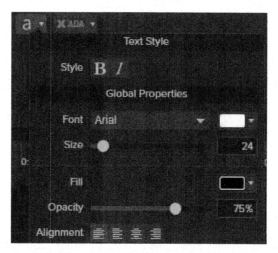

On the Canvas, the change to the font size is immediate. And you are likely thinking to yourself that the smaller font size looks much better than the clunky, larger font. However, keep in mind that the Captions aren't necessarily for you—they're for learners with a hearing disability. And when creating eLearning content, you'll need to be on the alert to anything you might do in your project that does not conform to the Americans with Disabilities Act (ADA).

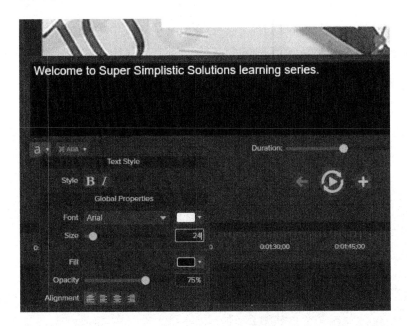

In case you're not familiar with ADA, it's a 1990 US civil rights law that prohibits discrimination against individuals with disabilities in all areas of public life, including jobs, schools, transportation, and all public and private places that are open to the general public. Generally speaking, the law exists to ensure that people with disabilities have the same rights and opportunities as everyone else and guarantees equal opportunity for individuals with disabilities in public accommodations, employment, transportation, state and local government services, and even eLearning.

In the image above, notice that Camtasia obeyed your formatting instructions without complaint and made the font size smaller. However, the smaller font size is no longer ADA-compliant. How would you know that? Check out the red X and ADA text below the Caption, an indication that you are not compliant.

4. Ensure font formatting is ADA-compliant.

   ❏ click the **ADA Compliance** drop-down menu and choose **Make Compliant**

The font size is restored to its larger size, which was ADA-compliant in the first place.

5. Add another Caption.

   ❑ on the **Timeline**, position the Playhead to the right of the first Caption

   ❑ click the **Add Caption** button

   ❑ in the space below the Canvas, type **This is lesson one: Creating New Folders.**

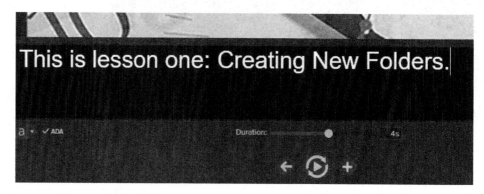

6. Preview the Callouts.

   ❑ on the Timeline, deselect all objects

   ❑ position the **Playhead** as far **left** as it can go

   ❑ on the **Canvas**, click the **Play** button to preview the lesson

With none of the Captions selected on the Timeline, you will get a fairly accurate preview of what learners see when they click the CC button on the Controller.

Notice that the timing of the captions does not exactly match the voiceover audio. You'll fix that next.

Student Activity: Control Caption Timing

1. Ensure that the **CaptionMe.tscproj** project is open.

2. Adjust Caption Timing

   ❑ on the **Timeline**, drag the **right** edge of the **first** Caption to the left a bit to shorten its play time

   ❑ on the **Timeline**, drag the **right** edge of the **second** Caption to the left a bit to shorten its play time

   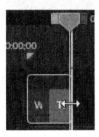

   ❑ on the Timeline, deselect all objects

   ❑ position the **Playhead** as far **left** as it can go

   ❑ on the **Canvas**, click the **Play** button to preview the lesson

   The Caption timing is a bit better but might still need work. You'll get a chance to tweak the timing a bit more and add another Caption during the Confidence Check that follows.

Captions Confidence Check

1. If the Caption timing needs it, spend a few moments making further adjustments.

2. Add a third Callout just to the right of the first two containing this text: **This lesson is going to teach you how to create a new folder on your computer.**

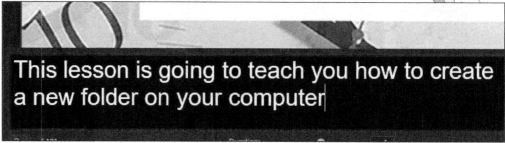

This lesson is going to teach you how to create a new folder on your computer

3. Preview the project from the beginning to see your new Caption.

4. If necessary, make adjustments to the Caption's timing so it matches the audio as closely as possible.

5. Share the project as a Local File. (Select Custom Production Settings.)

Custom production settings

6. Click the **Next** button twice.

7. When you get to the Smart Player Options, click the **Options** tab.

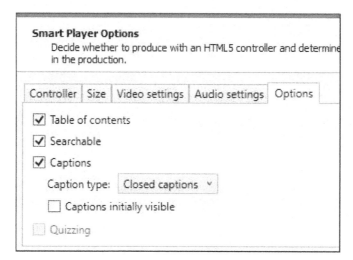

Smart Player Options
Decide whether to produce with an HTML5 controller and determine
in the production.

| Controller | Size | Video settings | Audio settings | Options |

☑ Table of contents

☑ Searchable

☑ Captions

   Caption type: Closed captions ˅

   ☐ Captions initially visible

☐ Quizzing

From this screen, you can enable or disable Captions and make their default state "visible" or "on by default." The standard practice is to make Captions not visible by default, so this option is fine as is.

8. Click the remaining **Next** buttons and the Finish button to finish the rendering process.

9. In the browser, click the **CC** button to view the Captions you added.

10. Close the browser window.

11. Back in Camtasia, close the Production Results window.

    Now you'll get a chance to copy and paste text from an existing voiceover script.

12. Minimize Camtasia and, from the **Camtasia9Data**, **Other_Assets** folder, open **CreatingFoldersVoiceoverScript**.

    Audio File 1:
    Welcome to Super Simplistic Solutions learning series.
    This is lesson one: Creating New Folders.

    Audio File 2:
    This lesson is going to teach you how to create a new folder on your computer, how to rename it, and how to both delete and restore recycled items.

    Audio File 3:
    When creating folders keep in mind that you can create as many folders as you need.

13. In the **Audio File 2** text, select **"how to rename it, and how to both delete and restore recycled items"** and copy the text to the Clipboard.

14. Return to Camtasia and the CaptionMe project.

15. Position the Playhead just to the right of your existing Captions.

16. Create a new Caption and paste the text you copied into the space beneath the Canvas.

17. Save your work.

Student Activity: Use Speech-to-Text to Create Closed Captions

1. Ensure that the **CaptionMe.tscproj** project is open.

2. Delete the existing Captions.

   ☐ on the **Timeline**, right-click the Captions on Track 4 and choose **Delete**

3. Create Captions using Speech-to-Text.

   ☐ from the list of tools at the left, click **Captions**

   ☐ from the upper left of the Captions panel, click **Script Options** (the **gear** icon)

   ☐ choose **Speech-to-Text**

You'll receive some tips for improving the Speech-to-Text feature. Later, after you've had a chance to work with Camtasia, you should try some of these tips and see how they might improve your Speech-to-Text results. For this activity, you're going to use the default settings to see where they take you.

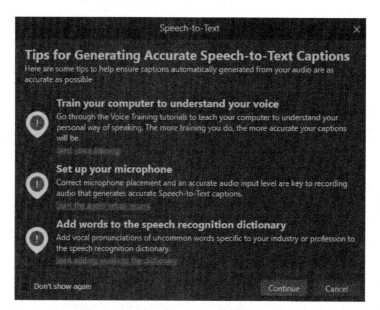

   ☐ click the **Continue** button

Camtasia listens to the voiceover audio in the background and, like magic, creates Captions on Track 4.

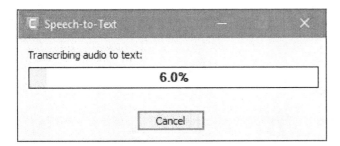

When you move through the Timeline, you'll see that not all of the Captions are ready to Share (you'd have to go through them and spend some time editing). However, most people who use this feature agree that it's faster to go this route than transcribe the audio from scratch.

> this lesson is going to teach you how to create a new folder a new computer Halloween name it and how both the leap and restore recycled

You've learned three ways to add Captions: transcribing, copy/paste, and Speech-to-Text. I've had the best luck using the copy/paste technique (that assumes you have a voiceover script that has already been created). I've also found that Speech-to-Text, given enough customization/tweaking, yields higher than average returns.

4. Save your project.

5. Exit Camtasia.

   And a hearty congratulations are in order... you have completed this book. You should now feel comfortable creating Camtasia projects from scratch, recording screen actions, and adding such Camtasia media and assets as videos, callouts, images, Behaviors, audio, quizzes, and captions. You should also feel comfortable in your ability to not only Share your content locally, but also on YouTube, Vimeo, and Screencast.com.

   I hope you enjoy using Camtasia to create eLearning as much as I do. Should you get stuck using Camtasia, the first place to look for help is online via the TechSmith Camtasia website (http://techsmith.com) and TechSmith blog (blogs.techsmith.com/category/tips-how-tos/). TechSmith has a great community offering free tips, tricks, and step-by-step videos.

Notes

Index

A
ADA, Make Compliant, 139
Add a Fill in the blank
 Question, 126
Add a timeline Marker, 112
Add a track, 50
Add a Video to the
 Timeline, 44
Add a Watermark to a
 Shared Video, 99
Add a Zoom-n-Pan, 109
Add Caption, 37
Add Effects While
 Recording, 38
Add quiz, 122
Add System Stamp, 37
Add to Timeline at
 Playhead, 44, 47
Add-ins, PowerPoint, 134
Advanced tab, 46
Animations, 109
Annotation tab, 33
Annotations, 14, 33, 60
Apple, 42
Arial, 8, 9
Ask for file name, 25
Association of Information
 Systems, 9
Attach Canvas, 20
Audio
 M4A, 72
 MP3, 72
 WAV, 72
 WMA, 72
Audio Effects, 74
Audio Files, import, 72
Audio Setup, 76
Auto Capture versus Manual
 Capture, 3, 12
Automatic file name, 25

B
Background Image,
 replace, 117
Background Music, add, 72
Behaviors, 65
Book Conventions, vi
Branching, 112

C
Calibri, 9
Callouts, 60
Camtasia Editor
 Interface, 12
Camtasia PowerPoint
 Add-in, 134
Camtasia Quiz Service, 132
Camtasia Recorder 9, 24

Camtasia Tools, 14
Canvas Options
 drop-down, 20
Caption Background
 Color, 35, 36
Caption Timing, 141
Captions, 137
 ADA Compliance, 139
 Add Caption
  button, 138, 140
 Font Properties, 138
 Speech-to-text, 137
Capture keyboard input, 25
Capture layered
 windows, 25
Capture settings, 25
Century Schoolbook, 9
Click to continue, 117
Clip Bin, 16
Codecs, 26
Countdown, 26
Course Projects, vii
Create Quizzes, 122
Credits and copyright clip, 3
Cursor Effects, 54, 55
Cursor effects, deleting, 56
Custom production
 settings, 99
Customize a TOC, 117
Cut a Segment of Unwanted
 Audio, 84

D
Data Files, vii
Default Capture options, 26
Delete cursor effects, 56
Designing Slides in
 Captivate, 7
Detach Canvas, 19
Development Process, 4
Disable screen saver during
 capture, 25
Display Resolution and
 Recording Area, 22
Do not show this again check
 boxes, 46
Duration, 59

E
eCommerce, 9
Edit Answer Details, 128
Editor, 13
Effects, 33, 38
Elapsed time, 33
E-Mail, ix
Export as Zip, 102
Extend Frame, 105
Extend play time, 52

F
Fade Audio In and Out, 74
Fade in button, 74
Fill In the Blank
 Question, 126
Fonts, 8
Fonts and eLearning, 8
Fonts and Learning, 8
Fonts, Most Popular, 9
Force popup dialogs into
 region, 26
Force popup dialogs into the
 recording area, 26
Force region to multiple of
 4, 26
Full screen, 29
Full Screen mode, 20

G
Ganga Dhanesh, 9
Getting Started Project, 12
Glow transition, 68
Glowing capture
 rectangle, 26
Go to frame at time, 117
Google Drive, 102
Group, Create, 58
Group, Rename, 59

H
Help, 12
Helvetica, 9
Hide preview window after
 recording is stopped, 27
Hotkeys, 27
Hotspots, 117
 Marker, 117
 Pause at End, 117
 Time, 117
 URL, 117
HTML options, 115
HTML5, 114

I
Image scale, 101
Import a voice narration, 80
Import Media, 42
Include all files from Media
 Bin in zip, 102
Include watermark, 99
Interactive Hotspot, 118
Interactivity, 122
Interface, 12

J
Jump to URL, 117

L
Left Click effects, 56
Library, 17
Linking Concerns, 102
Local File, 114
Location, Location, Location, 76
Lock a track, 77

M
Maker name, 112
Markers, Add, 112
Media Bin, 42
Microphone from the drop-down menu, 78
Microphone Placement, 76
Microphone Technique, 76
Microsoft, 10, 42
Minimize recorder, 27
Minimize t, 27
Minimize to system tray during recording, 27
More button, 137
MP3, 72
MP4, 114
MP4 - Smart Player (HTML5), 114, 117
MP4 Smart Player (HTML5), 99
MP4 with Smart Player, 96, 97
MPEG Audio Layer III, 72
Multiple Choice Question, 122
Multiple Choice Questions, 122
Mute timeline during recording, 78

N
Need More Books?, ix
New Projects, Creating, 42

O
Opacity, 53
Open Production Folder button, 93
Output file name area, 25

P
Palatino, 9
Pause before starting capture, 25
Personas, Fonts, 10
Planning eLearning, 3
Planning New Movies, 3, 12
Play/Pause, 52
Playhead, 45, 51
Playhead Snapping, 104
Popular Fonts, 9
PowerPoint, 134

PowerPoint Add-in, 134
Preferences, 46
Privacy, 95
Produce an AVI for CD Distribution, 94, 97
Produce Flash/HTML5 Output, 97, 99
Production Results dialog box, 93
Project Size, 6
Prompt before capture, 35
Properties, 53
Proprietary, 42

Q
Quick Time, 42
Quiz Options, 123, 124
Quizzes, 122
    Add to Timeline, 122
    Fill In the Blank, 126
    Fill in the Blank, 126
    Multiple Choice Question, 122
    Options, 123
    Quiz Question Properties, 124
    Score, 123
    See how Quiz looks in your viewer, 127
    Viewer can see their results, 123

R
Readability of Fonts, 9
Rec button, 31, 38
Record a Video, 31
Record audio, 28
Record screen after starting capture, 26
Record Voice Narration, 77
Record webcam, 28
Record/Pause, 27
Recorder control panel, 24
    Add caption, 37
    Add system stamp, 37
    Annotations, 37
    Menus, 24
    Options, 24
    REC button, 24
    Recorded inputs, 24
    Select area, 24
Recording Audio
    Microphone placement, 76
    Microphone technique, 76
    Monitor your audio level as you record, 76
    Setup, 76
Recording control panel, 24
Recording inputs, 24

Recording Size, 7
Remove from Timeline, 47
Remove Track, 59
Rename Group, 59
Rename Tracks, 84
Report dropped frames, 26
Report quiz results through email, 130
Require viewers to input name & email address, 130
Resolution and Recording Size, 12
Restore cursor location after pause, 26, 27
Restore defaults, 27
Round frame size to a 4-pixel boundary, 26

S
Sans Serif, 8
Screen Resolution, 3, 12
Screencast, 129
ScreenDraw, 38
Select a Recording Area, 29
Select color from image, 62
Serif, 8
Sharing projects with a buddy, 102
Show all tips, 46
Show countdown before recording, 26
Silence, 85
Silence Audio, 86
Skills Assessment, xii
Software updates and this book, ix
Speech-to-Text, 144
Stage, 19
Start recording, 78
Start Voice Recording button, 78
Stop Hotkey, 27
Super Simplistic Solutions, vii
System Caption, 33
System Stamp, 33
System Stamp position, 35

T
Table of contents, 114
Text Properties, 61, 62
Thumbnail view, 42
Thumbnails, 17
Time/date, 33
Timeline Marker, Add, 112
Times, 9
Times New Roman, 9
Tips, 46
Title clip, 3
TOC, Add, 114

Tracks, Adding, 50
Transitions, 68
    Add Slide Transitions, 68
    Add to a group, 68
    Add to Selected
       Media, 68
    Cube rotate, 68
    Modify Timing, 69
    Set Transition
       Duration, 69
    Wheel, 68
Transparent color, 100
TREC, 24
TREC Video, import, 42
Trust, Fonts, 9
TSCPROJ file, 45, 102
Typography, 9

U
Ungroup, 107

USB vs. Analog
    Microphones, 76
Use Trimmed Content in
    Transition, 69

V
Verdana, 8, 9
View Answers button, 128
Viewer identity, 130, 131
Vimeo, 102
Voice Narration, 14, 76, 78
Voice Narration panel, 14
Voiceover Scripts, 76

W
Watermark position, 100
Watermark, create, 53
Watermarks, 99
WAV, 72
WAVE, 72

Waveform, 72
Welcome window, 13
Where would you like to save
    your video files, 90
Windows Media Video, 42
WMA, 72

Y
YouTube Category, 95
YouTube Description, 94
YouTube Privacy, 95
YouTube Title, 94
YouTube, Share to, 94

Z
Zoom, 85
Zoom In, 47
Zoom Out, 47
Zoom-n-Pan, 109
Zoom-n-Pan mark, 109

ISBN 1-944607-00-5

53900

TechSmith Camtasia 9: The Essentials

CPSIA information can be obtained
at www.ICGtesting.com
Printed in the USA
FSOW04n1305160317
31990FS

9 781944 607012